D0214565

Wheat in the Third World

IADS DEVELOPMENT-ORIENTED
LITERATURE SERIES
Steven A. Breth, series editor

Wheat in the Third World
was prepared under the auspices of the
International Agricultural Development Service
with the participation and
financial support of the
International Maize and Wheat Improvement Center
and
The Rockefeller Foundation

ALSO IN THIS SERIES

*Rice in the Tropics: A Guide to the Development
of National Programs*, Robert F. Chandler, Jr.

*Small Farm Development: Understanding and Improving
Farming Systems in the Humid Tropics*, Richard R. Harwood

*Successful Seed Programs:
A Planning and Management Guide*, Johnson E. Douglas

Tomatoes in the Tropics, Ruben L. Villareal

Wheat in the Third World

Haldore Hanson,
Norman E. Borlaug, and
R. Glenn Anderson

Westview Press / Boulder, Colorado

IADS Development-Oriented Literature Series

Published in 1982 in the United States of America by
  Westview Press, Inc.
  5500 Central Avenue
  Boulder, Colorado 80301
  Frederick A. Praeger, President and Publisher

Library of Congress Cataloging in Publication Data
Hanson, Haldore E., 1912–
    Wheat in the Third World.
    (IADS development-oriented literature series)
    Prepared under the auspices of the International Agricultural Development Service.
    Bibliography: p.
    Includes index.
    1. Underdeveloped areas—Wheat. 2. Wheat. I. Borlaug, N. E. II. Anderson, Robert Glenn, 1924–1981. III. International Agricultural Development Service. IV. Title. V. Series.
    SB191.W5H27 1982   338.1'311'091724   82-8478
    ISBN 0-86531-357-1   AACR2

Printed and bound in the United States of America

Contents

List of Tables..ix
List of Figures...x
Foreword, A. Colin McClung.............................xi
Preface..xiii
Dedication... xvii

1. The Importance of Wheat and Its Principal
    Characteristics 1

    Wheat in the world's diet............................1
    Production and yields of wheat.......................3
    How environments affect wheat yields.................3
    Types of wheat.......................................9
    Protein content of wheat............................11
    Wheat preferences...................................13

2. The Modern Wheat Plant and the New
    Technology 15

    Traditional wheats..................................16
    Japanese dwarfs.....................................18
    Characteristics of semi-dwarf wheats................20
    New agronomic practices.............................22
    Disease control.....................................23
    The social impact of modern wheats..................26

3. Mexico: A Pioneer...................................29

    The postwar wheat situation.........................29
    The research program................................30
    Private support for agricultural research...........39

Training scientists. 39
Benefits of wheat research. 40
Mexico's future wheat imports. 42

4. India and Pakistan: The Asian Leaders. 43

India's wheat program. 43
Pakistan's wheat experience. 49
Supporting services for agriculture. 50
Controversies 52
Second-generation problems. 54
Some conclusions about India and Pakistan. 56

5. Turkey: A Dryland Success. 59

Turkey's wheat environments. 59
A revolution in three stages. 61
Overview of the revolution. 65
Some issues in the wheat revolution. 66
Looking ahead. 67

6. Bangladesh, China, Brazil, and Argentina. 69

BANGLADESH: A NEWCOMER TO WHEAT. 69

Modern varieties. 70
Factors of success. 71

CHINA: LARGEST WHEAT GROWER IN THE
      THIRD WORLD. 74

Distribution and types of wheat. 74
Wheat diseases. 74
Factors in China's wheat expansion. 75
And the future?. 78

BRAZIL: A PROGRAM WITH EXTREME SOIL
      AND DISEASE PROBLEMS. 79

Acid soils. 79
Septoria and scab. 81
A cost/benefit question. 81

ARGENTINA: A MAJOR EXPORTER. 82

7. Elements of an Effective National Wheat
    Program..83

    Joining a wheat network.......................83
    Identifying wheat-growing zones...............85
    Problem-oriented research with a team approach.......86
    Plant quarantine service......................91
    Availability of inputs........................92
    Agricultural extension........................97
    Economic policies............................100
    Dealing with an oversupply of wheat..........103
    Farmers' service organizations...............106
    Psychological factors........................106
    The dynamic program leader...................107

8. Postharvest Wheat Handling....................109

    Harvesting and threshing.....................109
    Cleaning.....................................111
    Drying.......................................111
    Marketing....................................112
    Handling and transporting....................112
    Storage......................................113
    Milling and grading..........................116
    Commercial bakeries..........................117
    Composite flour..............................118
    Wheat for feed and industrial use............118

9. Promising Wheat Research for the Future.......119

    YIELD DEPENDABILITY..........................119

    Resistance to rusts..........................122
    Other weapons against rusts..................122
    Resistance to other fungus diseases..........124
    Tolerance to environmental stress............126

    NARROWING THE YIELD GAP......................127

    Supplying nutrients..........................128
    Weed control.................................130
    Insecticides and fungicides..................132

Timely production practices.........................132

ON-FARM RESEARCH............................133

RAISING THE YIELD POTENTIAL...................135
Crossing spring wheats with winter wheats...........135
Longer heads, more spikelets, more fertile florets......137
Durum wheat research............................138
Triticale: A wide cross...........................139
Other wide crosses..............................139

10. Prospects for Wheat in the 1980s and 1990s..........141

World population growth.........................141
Land pressure..................................143
Fertilizer production outlook.....................144
Outlook for wheat in international trade.............146
Can wheat maintain its share in the developing
    world's diet?...............................148

Appendix: Where to Get Wheat Assistance.............151
Glossary 155
Annotated Bibliography..........................160
Index..170

Tables

1. World food production, 1979.........................2

2. Area, production, and yield of wheat in major
   producing countries, 1978–1980......................4

3. Some spring bread-wheat varieties released in
   Mexico...32

4. Some durum varieties released in Mexico.............33

5. Impact of weather upon wheat yields on the
   Anatolian plateau of Turkey........................65

6. Turkey: Wheat production and input use for all
   crops, 1946–1979...................................66

7. Bangladesh: Wheat expansion and
   imports, 1961–1980.................................70

8. Checklist of elements in an effective wheat-
   production program.................................84

9. The CIMMYT crossing block, 1981: Outstanding
   varieties used as sources of selected spring
   bread-wheat characteristics........................89

10. Major fungus diseases of bread wheat in
    developing countries..............................120

11. Population projections in selected wheat-growing
    countries...142

12. Population pressure in selected wheat-growing
    countries, 1980 and 2000..........................145

13. Major wheat-trading countries.....................147

Figures

1. A productivity ladder illustrating a range of wheat yields..6

2. Wheat yields in four environments......................8

3. Response to fertilizer of two short varieties and one tall variety of wheat...........................21

4. Mexico's wheat-growing areas........................30

5. Annual average wheat area, yield, and production in Mexico................................34

6. India's wheat-growing areas.........................46

7. Turkey's wheat-growing areas........................60

8. China's wheat-growing areas.........................75

9. Brazil's wheat-growing areas........................80

10. Changes in population and wheat production in developing countries, 1961–1979.................149

Foreword

The new short-wheat varieties that began moving from Mexico to other developing countries in the 1960s were the vanguard of the green revolution. With their wide adaptation, resistance to rusts, and responsiveness to fertilizer, those wheats had a far-reaching impact on agriculture in developing countries. They gave researchers an impetus to develop new farm practices and to launch intensive breeding programs aimed at combining the best features of local and imported varieties. For farmers, the potentially handsome returns offered by short varieties made it worthwhile to learn and apply new farming techniques. For farsighted policymakers, the new wheats were a rallying point for strengthening agricultural research capabilities and improving credit availability, input supplies, and other services necessary to a productive agriculture.

Nonetheless, with rapidly rising populations in most developing nations, the struggle is far from over. Rich rewards are available to nations that marshal their resources to improve wheat production through modern research, improved methods of testing and transferring technology, and more efficient services to farmers.

Wheat in the Third World, like other books developed by the International Agricultural Development Service for the Development-Oriented Literature Series, is primarily aimed at decision makers who influence the course of agriculture in developing countries. These decision makers are a heterogeneous group: They are found, obviously, in ministries of agriculture and national wheat improvement programs, but also in planning commissions, credit agencies, rural development projects, extension services, international assistance agencies, and development banks. We hope the information this book contains will help them in their efforts to eradicate malnutrition.

This book results from a collaboration by three respected international authorities. Haldore Hanson was the director general of

CIMMYT (International Maize and Wheat Improvement Center) from 1972 to 1978 and earlier was the Ford Foundation representative in Nigeria and Pakistan. Norman Borlaug began doing research in wheat in Mexico in 1943 under a program sponsored by the Ministry of Agriculture and the Rockefeller Foundation. When CIMMYT was founded, he became the first director of the wheat program, in which post he served until his retirement in 1979. In recognition of his exceptional contributions to the battle against world hunger, he received the Nobel Peace Prize in 1970. The late Glenn Anderson was appointed director of the wheat program in 1979 after having served as associate director since 1971. Dr. Anderson had previously been joint coordinator of the All-India Coordinated Wheat Improvement Project.

IADS gratefully acknowledges the support of CIMMYT and the Rockefeller Foundation in the development of this book.

A. Colin McClung
President
International Agricultural Development Service

Arlington, Virginia

Preface

This book is written for administrators and policymakers in developing countries. In preparing the manuscript, we assumed that the reader holds a responsibility related to wheat in a developing country — for research and extension, for the distribution of inputs like fertilizer or irrigation water, for the operation of storage or milling facilities, for establishing prices for flour, for budgeting for agriculture, or for planning national food security.

Some readers will be nonscientists; therefore, the presentation minimizes the use of technical language and defines technical terms. Because administrators have crowded schedules and their reading time is limited, the book is brief and omits details that are available in longer accounts.

Chapter 1 sets the stage by describing the principal characteristics of wheat. Chapter 2 recounts the development of "modern wheat" and new technology since World War II and describes the social impact of modern wheat. Chapters 3 to 6 describe national wheat programs — a body of information that until now has been scattered in newspapers and journals. Three countries are given fuller treatment: Mexico, because it pioneered new patterns of wheat research and helped create an international network of scientists; India, because it tripled its wheat production in 15 years and doubled its national wheat yields, thus making itself self-sufficient in wheat and demonstrating many of the steps other countries need to follow to organize a successful national wheat program; and Turkey, a low-rainfall country with little irrigation, which developed new dryland practices that helped raise its annual wheat harvest by 70 percent in 10 years, thus ending a long period of wheat deficits and creating an exportable surplus. Other national programs are presented more briefly: Pakistan, Bangladesh, China, Brazil, and Argentina, each illustrating special accomplishments. Collectively the eight studies offer experiences on most problems that national wheat programs in developing countries will meet.

Chapter 7 draws upon the eight case studies to state the authors' conclusions on the elements of an effective national production program. Chapter 8 describes postharvest technology. Chapter 9 looks at promising future wheat-research subjects and offers some research guidelines for administrators. Chapter 10 closes with some comments on the future of wheat in relation to population growth, the pressure of man on the land, fertilizer supplies, and world trade.

Technical libraries contain many books and journals on wheat, but so vast a range of reading material is not helpful to the decision makers in developing countries who wish to know what are the characteristics of the crop, what is the modern wheat plant, what are the elements of an effective production campaign, what are the successes and difficulties experienced by other countries, and what is the outlook for wheat over the next 10 or 20 years. Providing concise answers to these questions is the role this book aims to fill.

The authors of this book have all been associated with the International Maize and Wheat Improvement Center, an organization in Mexico generally referred to by its Spanish acronym CIMMYT. CIMMYT is engaged in agricultural research, training, and consulting for developing countries, and its wheat activities are described in the Appendix.

The "Mexican wheat program"—often referred to in the pages that follow—began in 1943 as a joint research and training effort between the Mexican Ministry of Agriculture and the Rockefeller Foundation. Initially this was a national program aiming to benefit only Mexico, but gradually wheat lines and varieties developed in Mexico were distributed to other countries, especially in South America and southern Asia. By 1960 it had become desirable to create a separate Mexican agricultural research institute, the Instituto Nacional de Investigaciones Agricolas (INIA), and to reorganize the international agricultural activities into a new service body, which since 1966 has been called CIMMYT.

CIMMYT's home base is in Mexico. It benefits from Mexico's broad range of agricultural climates and uses the facilities of some Mexican national research stations. The Mexican Ministry of Agriculture conducts its own wheat testing and seed multiplication programs. The sister institutions—INIA for Mexico and CIMMYT for the developing world—continue to exchange germ plasm and technology, but each institution is autonomous.

The term *Mexican program* throughout this book refers to the combined breeding and agronomic testing of the Mexican Ministry of Agriculture and CIMMYT. The close collaboration among CIMMYT, the Mexican government, and a world wheat network has been a major factor in the progress achieved.

Haldore Hanson
Norman E. Borlaug
R. Glenn Anderson

El Batan, Mexico

R. Glenn Anderson, 1924–1981. (*Source:* CIMMYT.)

Dedication

Glenn Anderson was a big man in physique, in intellect, and in personal warmth. He crowded more into a lifetime of 57 years than others who have lived many years longer. After earning a doctorate at the University of Saskatchewan, Glenn broadened his grasp of science as a university professor, then applied that knowledge as a geneticist and plant breeder for the Canadian Department of Agriculture. By age 40, he was co-leader of India's national wheat program, the largest and perhaps the most remarkable in the developing world. From there, Glenn rose to a position of leadership in a world network of wheat scientists and assumed the direction of CIMMYT's international wheat program 2 years before he died in February 1981. This man was never happier than when walking through the wheat fields of a developing country, surrounded by a group of local scientists, and tactfully pointing out the problems that needed attention.

Glenn Anderson spent his boyhood on a small unmechanized grain/livestock farm in Ontario, where he engaged in hard physical labor and experienced the privations of the world depression of the 1930s. He learned from direct exposure the disappointments of an adverse climate and poor soil. But he also found in those early years what science could do for farmers, and he devoted his adult years to the development and spread of technology that could provide a base for prosperous farming.

Glenn Anderson was one of the authors of this book. As in all his activities, he gave much of his time and knowledge. He was the main author of several portions of the book: the pages on India, a country he regarded as his second home; the story of Bangladesh, a country Glenn greatly admired and to which he gave much thought; and the chapter on future research, a favorite topic for Anderson, the planner.

A draft manuscript had already been completed when Glenn Anderson's career ended abruptly. His vision, work ethic, and scientific imagination inspired many of his colleagues, and through them his work goes on.

This book is dedicated to Glenn Anderson.

1
The Importance of Wheat and Its Principal Characteristics

Wheat is special in several ways.

First, wheat is grown on 240 million hectares, an area larger than that of any other crop.

Second, wheat contributes more calories and more protein to the world's diet than any other food crop.

Third, world trade in wheat exceeds trade in all other grains combined.

Fourth, the raised bread loaf is possible because the wheat kernel contains gluten, an elastic form of protein. When leavened dough ferments, the gluten traps minute bubbles of carbon dioxide, which make the dough rise.

Fifth, winter wheats (wheats of winter habit) possess a combination of genes that in temperate climates permits the wheats to be seeded and to germinate in the autumn; to survive winter temperatures as low as $-30°C$, usually under snow cover; and to grow, flower, and mature rapidly before hot, drying summer winds occur. (Spring wheats, a second major group of wheats, can be sown in any season if temperature and moisture conditions are suitable, but they cannot survive cold winters.)

Wheat in the world's diet

The world's diet is shown in Table 1. In the table, gross output is converted to an edible dry-matter basis because of the wide variation in moisture content among the various commodities. For example, starchy roots average 73 percent moisture, but cereals average only 12 percent.

Plants constitute 93 percent of the world's diet. Cereals contribute two thirds of all food, and among the cereals, wheat is the

Table 1
World food production, 1979

Commodity	Production (million tons)		
	Gross	Edible dry matter[a]	Protein[a]
Cereals	1,553	1,293	134
wheat	425	374	44
maize	394	347	36
rice, rough	380	258	22
barley	172	151	15
sorghum/millet	100	89	8
Roots and tubers	548	148	9
potato	284	62	6
sweet potato	114	34	2
cassava	117	43	1
Legumes, oilseeds, nuts	221	147	50
Sugarcane and sugar beets (sugar content only)	102	102	0
Vegetables and melons	340	41	4
Fruits	287	37	2
Animal products	699	135	58
milk, meat, eggs	624	115	43
fish	75	20	14
All food	3,750	1,903	257

[a]At zero moisture content, excluding inedible hulls and shells.

Sources: FAO *Production yearbook;* UN *Statistical yearbook:* FAO *State of food and agriculture, 1964;* correspondence. Format adapted from L. T. Evans, ed., 1975, *Crop physiology.*

largest crop. Animal products, which make up the remaining 7 percent of the world's diet, of course come indirectly from plants — cereals and forages. About two fifths of the world's cereal output is fed to animals, according to the U.S. Department of Agriculture, and to that extent, cereals are double counted in Table 1. But in developing countries, only 9 percent of the grain used is fed to animals.

Of the total protein production, three quarters comes from plants. Wheat alone contributes the same amount of protein as all meat, milk, and eggs.

Fish make up only 1 percent of the world's diet, even though water covers 71 percent of the earth's surface. The widely prophesied bounty of the sea has not yet begun to be realized.

Production and yields of wheat

The production of major wheat-growing countries is summarized in Table 2. The progress during the last 18 years, which includes the first introductions of modern short wheats, is shown as annual percentage change. During this period, average wheat yields in all developing countries rose from 944 kg/ha to 1300 kg/ha; the area of wheat planted rose from 76 million to 102 million hectares; and production doubled to 143 million tons. In comparison the population of all developing countries increased only 50 percent during the period.

Despite recent progress, however, wheat yields in developing countries lag behind those of industrialized countries, which in 1979 averaged 2200 kg/ha. This gap suggests opportunities for continued progress in future years.

How environments affect wheat yields

The potential yield a wheat farmer is capable of attaining is limited by the environment in the form of moisture, temperature, soil, and pests. These limitations should guide the kinds of research a government undertakes for each wheat environment and should influence the recommendations a government makes to farmers. Unless an administrator is well informed about the environmental constraints the farmer faces, recommendations are likely to be unrealistic.

The powerful influence of environment is shown in Figure 1, in which an assortment of yield data is arranged in a "yield ladder." The yields range from 400 kg/ha for rainfed wheat grown with unimproved technology to a theoretical high of 20,000 kg/ha—the level that some plant physiologists think should be possible under optimum sunlight, moisture, and soil fertility. This yield level has never been reached.

Table 2
Area, production, and yield of wheat in major producing countries, 1978–1980, and change in previous 18 years (annual averages)

Country	Area		Production		Yield	
	Avg. 1978–1980 (000 ha)	Change since 1960–1962 (%/yr)	Avg. 1978–1980 (000 tons)	Change since 1960–1962 (%/yr)	Avg. 1978–1980 (kg/ha)	Change since 1960–1962 (%/yr)
			Developing countries[a]			
Mexico	717	-0.7	2,427	3.3	3,385	3.9
Egypt	574	-0.3	1,862	1.2	3,244	1.4
Korea, DPR	150	-0.4	350	7.9	2,333	8.2
China	29,167	0.8	57,833	6.1	1,983	5.3
Bangladesh	303	9.3	553	15.5	1,825	6.2
Chile	562	-1.7	952	-0.5	1,694	1.2
Argentina	4,741	1.0	8,000	2.4	1,687	1.3
Turkey	8,600	0.6	13,367	3.8	1,554	3.2
India	22,019	2.8	32,940	6.0	1,496	3.2
Pakistan	6,650	1.8	9,691	5.0	1,457	3.2
Kenya	115	0.9	165	2.7	1,435	1.8
Nepal	307	4.6	353	5.5	1,150	0.9
Uruguay	274	-2.8	308	-1.6	1,124	1.2
Morocco	1,708	0.5	1,828	3.8	1,070	3.3
Afghanistan	2,250	0	2,400	0.3	1,067	0.3
Iran	4,850	2.0	5,100	3.5	1,052	1.6
Syria	1,539	0.4	1,619	3.3	1,052	2.9
Mongolia	360	0.8	367	2.7	1,019	1.9

Peru	95	-2.7	92	-2.8	968	-0.1
Libya	120	-1.0	106	6.5	883	7.4
Sudan	220	14.6	190	10.8	864	3.7
Brazil	3,257	6.5	2,690	7.8	826	1.3
Tunisia	1,047	0	785	4.4	750	4.4
Ethiopia	555	-2.8	401	-2.7	723	0
Iraq	1,665	1.0	1,030	1.1	619	0.2
Jordan	120	-4.5	72	-1.7	600	2.8
Algeria	2,100	0.8	1,166	-0.3	555	-1.1
Developed countries[b]						
France	4,270	0	21,305	3.4	4,989	3.5
Germany, FR	1,638	1.0	8,112	3.4	4,952	2.4
Yugoslavia	1,587	1.4	4,989	2.1	3,144	3.5
Poland	1,670	1.0	4,872	3.5	2,917	2.5
Italy	3,439	-1.5	9,029	0.5	2,625	2.0
Romania	2,226	-1.6	5,625	2.1	2,527	3.7
United States	25,617	1.4	56,972	3.0	2,224	1.6
Spain	2,663	-2.4	4,942	1.3	1,856	3.7
Canada	10,724	0.2	19,154	2.4	1,786	2.2
USSR	60,627	-0.3	100,340	2.2	1,655	2.5
Australia	10,941	3.3	14,936	3.8	1,365	0.5
South Africa	1,770	1.5	1,792	4.6	1,012	3.1

[a]With over 100,000 hectares of wheat.

[b]With over 1.5 million hectares of wheat.

Source: U.S. Dept. of Agriculture, *Reference tables.*

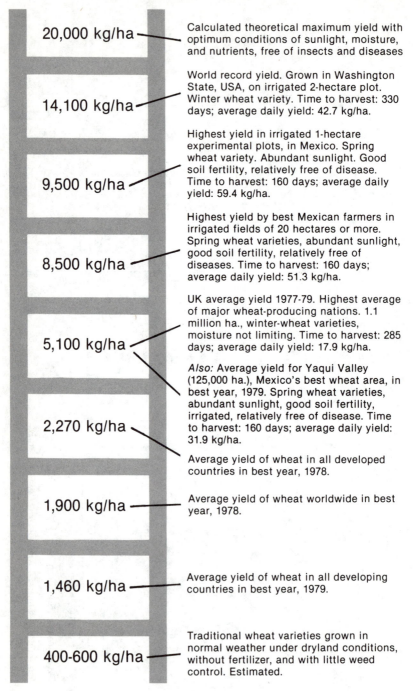

20,000 kg/ha — Calculated theoretical maximum yield with optimum conditions of sunlight, moisture, and nutrients, free of insects and diseases

14,100 kg/ha — World record yield. Grown in Washington State, USA, on irrigated 2-hectare plot. Winter wheat variety. Time to harvest: 330 days; average daily yield: 42.7 kg/ha.

9,500 kg/ha — Highest yield in irrigated 1-hectare experimental plots, in Mexico. Spring wheat variety. Abundant sunlight. Good soil fertility, relatively free of disease. Time to harvest: 160 days; average daily yield: 59.4 kg/ha.

8,500 kg/ha — Highest yield by best Mexican farmers in irrigated fields of 20 hectares or more. Spring wheat varieties, abundant sunlight, good soil fertility, relatively free of diseases. Time to harvest: 160 days; average daily yield: 51.3 kg/ha.

5,100 kg/ha — UK average yield 1977-79. Highest average of major wheat-producing nations. 1.1 million ha., winter-wheat varieties, moisture not limiting. Time to harvest: 285 days; average daily yield: 17.9 kg/ha.

Also: Average yield for Yaqui Valley (125,000 ha.), Mexico's best wheat area, in best year, 1979. Spring wheat varieties, abundant sunlight, good soil fertility, irrigated, relatively free of disease. Time to harvest: 160 days; average daily yield: 31.9 kg/ha.

2,270 kg/ha — Average yield of wheat in all developed countries in best year, 1978.

1,900 kg/ha — Average yield of wheat worldwide in best year, 1978.

1,460 kg/ha — Average yield of wheat in all developing countries in best year, 1979.

400-600 kg/ha — Traditional wheat varieties grown in normal weather under dryland conditions, without fertilizer, and with little weed control. Estimated.

Figure 1. A productivity ladder illustrating a range of wheat yields from various environments and under various levels of management.

Environment is the first limiting factor on every step of the yield ladder. The skill of the farmer comes second. When a favorable environment and a farmer's skill combine, as they did when the world's record wheat crop was grown in 1964–1965, the results can be astonishing. The record yield shown in Figure 1 was achieved with atypical production practices at a cost that is uneconomic for the ordinary farmer. As reported by R. H. Hageman, a farmer in Kittitas County, Washington State (U.S.A.), planted the winter-wheat variety Gaines in an irrigated 2-hectare plot in October 1964. Eleven months later, he harvested a publicly measured 14,100 kg/ha. The yield was approximately double the yield neighboring farmers obtained with the same variety, and it was eight times the average wheat yield in the United States that year.

The reasons for this record yield are not fully understood. There are however a number of contributing factors. The field had been reclaimed from wild sagebrush 2 years earlier. The soil was a rich loess; it was high in organic matter, had good tilth, and was free of root rot pathogens. In each of the first 2 years after the brush had been cleared, the land had been planted to maize and fertilized with 124 kg/ha of nitrogen. In the third year, wheat was seeded at 90 to 95 kg/ha. The wheat was fertilized at 135-25-56 (kilograms of nutrient nitrogen, phosphorus, and potassium per hectare). The crop was irrigated seven times between April and July 1965, receiving more applications and larger quantities of water than is the usual practice for the area. Finally, environmental conditions were optimum during much of the growing season—clear days with bright sunlight and cool nights.

The record grain crop was equal to 12, 238 kg/ha of dry matter that contained 250 kg/ha of nitrogen, 46 kg/ha of phosphorus, and 55 kg/ha of potassium. Since the crop took up from the soil more nutrients than the farmer applied, the accumulation of chemicals and organic matter in the soil provided the balance.

Another way of looking at the effect of environment and its interaction with farmers' skills is to compare wheat-growing areas. Figure 2 shows the influence of environment on wheat yields in four areas: Tunisia, Queensland in Australia, the Yaqui Valley of the State of Sonora in Mexico, and the United Kingdom. Of the four areas, Tunisia, with more than a million hectares of spring wheat, suffers the most severe limitations of environment (notably low rainfall) and attains the lowest average yields, about 500

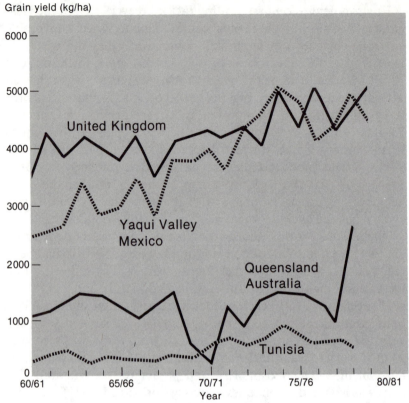

Figure 2. Wheat yields in four environments during two decades. (*Sources:* FAO; Bureau of Agricultural Economics, Canberra, Australia; CIANO, Ciudad Obregón, Mexico.)

kg/ha. Queensland, Australia, with 900,000 hectares of spring wheat, is limited by uncertain rainfall, but skilled farmers nevertheless achieve average wheat yields of 1000 to 2000 kg/ha. The Yaqui Valley in Mexico produces 125,000 hectares of spring wheat in a climate similar to that of Queensland, but the Yaqui Valley wheat is fully irrigated, and average yields have been as high as 5100 kg/ha. The United Kingdom produces 1.1 million hectares of winter-habit wheat in a growing season that averages 9½ months. Yield now exceeds 5000 kg/ha. The United Kingdom receives adequate rainfall, and its farmers are skilled managers and are among the world's heaviest users of chemical fertilizer.

Types of wheat

Wheats are commonly classified according to species, commercial type, and growth habit. There are 16 species, two principal commercial types, and three distinctive growth habits of wheat.

Species

The principal cereals eaten by man — wheat, rice, maize, barley, sorghum, millet, rye, and oats — are all seeds of plants that belong to the grass family, the *Gramineae*. Within the grass family, wheats are further classified under the genus *Triticum*. Within the genus *Triticum*, 16 species of wheat are commonly recognized, but only 2 species, *Triticum aestivum* and *Triticum durum*, are cultivated on a large scale.

Commercial types

Bread wheat and durum wheat are the two principal commercial types of wheat. Bread wheat (*Triticum aestivum*) covers about 90 percent of the world wheat area and makes up about 94 percent of harvest. Durum wheat (*T. durum*), sometimes called macaroni wheat, covers about 9 percent of the wheat area but constitutes only about 5 percent of the world's wheat harvest. Minor species of wheat, of which club wheat (*T. compactum*) is the most important, account for the remaining area and production.

Bread wheat or its ancestors were widely grown in the Fertile Crescent area of the Mideast 5000 to 6000 years ago. It gradually became the principal type of wheat in western Asia and Europe and spread eastward to India, China, and Japan. It was carried to the Western Hemisphere and to Australia and New Zealand by explorers and colonizers and thus encircled the world. Bread wheat is consumed in many forms: as noodles in Japan and China, as a kind of pancake (chapati in India and tortilla in Mexico), as flatbreads in South and Southwest Asia, as leavened breads and rolls in Europe and most countries where Europeans have migrated, and as porridge wherever wheat is grown.

Durum varieties are considered to be better adapted to low-rainfall areas than are bread-wheat varieties. Because the durum wheats tend to be grown in semi-arid climates, the average yield of durums is lower than that of bread wheats. Under irrigation, however, modern durum varieties yield as well as the highest-yielding bread wheats.

The kernels of durum wheat are typically larger, heavier, and harder than those of bread wheats. Durum dough is less elastic than that of bread wheat and therefore inferior for producing leavened loaves. But durum wheat is often used for noodles and other pasta products such as macaroni, spaghetti, and ravioli. Pasta products made from durum have a greater stability when cooked—they do not tend to disintegrate, to become sticky when boiled, or to become mushy if kept in water after cooking. In international trade, durums of good quality generally command a higher price than bread wheats.

Growth-habit classification

Prior to the beginning of agriculture, wheats evolved into two large gene pools—the winter-habit wheats and the spring-habit wheats—and a third, smaller pool, the facultative wheats. The terms *winter wheat* and *spring wheat* have a broader meaning than the season in which the crop is grown.

Winter-habit wheats are sown in the autumn. The seedlings usually emerge and tiller (produce extra stems) before winter; then they pass through an inactive stage during the cold weather. The plants resume rapid growth in the spring and mature in the summer after a total growing period of 9 to 11 months. Winter-habit wheats require vernalization (exposure to at least several weeks of temperatures between 1 and 5°C) before they can change from the grasslike vegetative stage to the reproductive phase, which includes jointing, heading, flowering, and setting seed. In the areas where they are sown, the active growth of winter-wheat varieties coincides with favorable moisture availability in autumn and spring. Moreover winter wheats tend to mature before the onset of the hot, dry summer winds that are characteristic of areas of continental climate.

Spring wheats, by contrast, have a continuous growth cycle—generally 3 to 6 months—and no inactive period. They cannot survive sustained low temperatures. In areas that have severe winters, they are planted in the spring after the last killing frost. In other areas, notably those with a Mediterranean climate, they are planted in the autumn and grow through the mild winter.

The two large gene pools possess other differences. Many winter wheats carry resistance to diseases that are common in the winter-wheat environment, such as powdery mildew, stripe rust, and septoria. Some winter wheats have a greater tolerance to drought than spring wheats. On the other hand, spring wheats have better resistance to stem rust and loose smut. Both pools carry some genes for high yield, and these genes appear to be distinct in character and sometimes additive when intercrossed.

Facultative wheats are intermediate in cold tolerance between winter wheats and spring wheats. Unlike the winter wheats, however, they do not require vernalization in order to flower and set seed.

We estimate that 40 percent of the world wheat area is sown to winter-habit wheats and produces 50 percent of the grain. Spring-habit wheats, we estimate, occupy 57 percent of the wheat area; the facultative type, no more than 3 percent.

Most wheat grown in developing countries is of spring growth habit. China and Turkey, however, are large growers of winter-habit wheats. Facultative wheats are grown in China, Turkey, Algeria, Iran, Afghanistan, Argentina, and Chile, but in relatively small amounts. In developed countries, which tend to have colder climates, winter-habit wheats predominate.

Protein content of wheat

Wheat compares well with other cereals in nutrient values. Its protein content is higher than that of rice, maize, and sorghum and about equal to that of other cereals. Protein content is influenced by wheat variety and by environmental and cultural conditions (such as temperature, moisture, methods of cultivation, type of soil, and availability of nitrogen).

Protein percentage in wheat can be manipulated to some extent by the amount of fertilizer applied and the timing of application. Applying nitrogen to the soil early in the crop season (before flowering) will generally result in higher grain yield, and applying nitrogen at flowering time or a little later will generally produce more protein in the grain but will have little effect upon yield.

The nutritional value of proteins is determined not only by the quantity of proteins, but by the balance of amino acids within the proteins. During human digestion, the proteins are broken down into their constituent parts, which are absorbed into the bloodstream and then reassemble to form different kinds of proteins needed by the body for growth or for maintenance and repair. Eight amino acids are called "essential" for adults (10 for infants) because the human body cannot manufacture them and must obtain them from food. The biological value of the protein of a food like wheat is set by the first limiting essential amino acid, that is, the amino acid that falls short of the body's requirements to the greatest extent. In wheat, the first limiting amino acid is lysine.

There are two problems with lysine in wheat protein. First, when wheat is milled, a third of the total protein and lysine in whole wheat is removed. The loss occurs because much of the protein and much of the lysine are located in the bran and in the germ, which are separated from the flour during milling. Breeders have not been able to change the way protein and lysine are apportioned among the various parts of the grain. Second, high-protein wheats generally contain higher quantities of the proteins that form gluten, which is low in lysine. There tends to be an inverse ratio between the amount of protein in the grain and the amount of lysine per gram of protein.

Protein improvement has rarely been a major objective of wheat breeders because wheat protein has usually been considered adequate for human nutrition. But the discovery of special genes that elevate the quantity of lysine in maize, sorghum, and barley stimulated a search for similar genes in wheat in the 1970s. None were discovered that are comparable to the high-lysine genes of those other cereals, but breeders are still seeking to identify minor variations in the lysine content of wheat and to pyramid these variations into superior varieties.

At the University of Nebraska (U.S.A.), an outstanding group of wheat breeders and biochemists searched the world collections of both winter and spring wheats in the hope of finding lines that would raise lysine levels and thus improve the nutritional quality of wheat. They succeeded in identifying breeding materials that contained elevated protein, gave competitive grain yields, and did not suffer a depression of lysine, which is commonly associated with increased protein. One winter-wheat variety has been released from this program.

Wheat preferences

Farmers, millers, bakers, and consumers differ in their concepts of desirable qualities in wheat. To farmers, a variety of wheat has "quality" if it resists diseases, matures at the proper time, does not topple over before harvest, and gives a good yield of plump grains without shattering (grains falling to the ground before harvest). The miller is concerned with the grain. The kernels should be uniform, the grain should be free of foreign matter, the moisture content should be low and the protein content high, and the yield of flour per 100 kilograms of wheat should be high. The baker who produces leavened bread looks for flour that produces dough with desirable characteristics: The dough should be able to hold gas bubbles and yield a large loaf with good internal texture and color. The consumer does not see wheat grain before it is milled, but he or she has strong preferences regarding the appearance, texture, aroma, and flavor of the breads, biscuits, cakes and other products that trace their character partly to the wheat kernels. These differing viewpoints of farmer, miller, baker, and consumer must all be considered by a government that sets out to raise its wheat production.

The Modern Wheat Plant and the New Technology

Since World War II, more progress has been made in raising wheat yields of developing countries than occurred in the preceding 8,000 to 10,000 years that followed domestication of the crop. In 1950 the average wheat yield in developing countries was about 700 kg/ha, but by 1979 it had risen to 1450 kg/ha.

This acceleration of progress stems from at least three causes. First, during the 1960s and 1970s, plant breeders developed new wheats that were shorter in stature, higher yielding, earlier to mature, more resistant to diseases, and more responsive to fertilizers. Second, use of fertilizers and irrigation expanded greatly. Third, agronomists worked out suitable production practices for the new wheats—methods of sowing, irrigating, fertilizing, conserving moisture, and controlling weeds. Cereal chemists studied the protein content of the new varieties and their milling and baking qualities. Engineers developed simple implements to level the land and to plant seeds at the recommended density and soil depth, to till the soil while conserving moisture, to apply fertilizer more effectively, and to thresh the grain by more efficient methods than the old-fashioned animal trampling and hand winnowing. Economists studied the impact of new technology on rural employment, on the distribution of farm income, and on patterns of nutrition (because profitable new wheats were invading lands previously devoted to other crops and were thus modifying national diets).

The new wheat technology was created by groupings, or networks, of scientists in more than 100 countries. A network of scientists conducts trials on superior experimental varieties developed by participants in the group. CIMMYT (the International Maize and Wheat Improvement Center, in Mexico) and

ICARDA (International Center for Agricultural Research in Dry Areas, in Syria) serve as centers for mixing wheat germ plasm, shipping nurseries, publishing data, training participant scientists, and consulting on production problems (see Appendix). The breeding work attributed to Mexico is the work of a multinational team. The CIMMYT wheat staff, in 1979, consisted of 34 scientists and fellows of 17 nationalities including 5 Mexicans, 5 Africans, 5 Asians, 5 Europeans, 2 South Americans, 2 Australians, 2 Canadians, and 8 U.S. nationals.

Traditional wheats

The traditional wheat plant is tall (typically 125 to 150 centimeters) and has a weak stem, or stalk. As it grows and manufactures carbohydrates, it deposits a large amount of its dry matter in the stem and leaves in relation to the amount in the grain.

Traditional wheats have some attributes for cultivation under poor farming conditions. When weed control is inadequate, tall plants can survive by overshadowing most weeds. In infertile soils, tall plants tend to give sparse stands, and the relatively wide spacing between plants creates a microclimate in the grainfield that is unfavorable for the multiplication of diseases and insects. Consequently, although the yields of the old tall plants are low, they are fairly dependable despite poor management.

In the early post–World War II years, scientists tried to raise wheat yields by applying fertilizers, but the results were not as favorable as anticipated. Nitrogen applied to tall plants causes them to grow even taller and leafier, and they tend to lodge (fall over) before maturity, thus depressing yields. In fact, the more nitrogen applied above about 50 kg/ha of N, the earlier the plants lodge, and the greater the yield depression. Moreover fertilizing the tall traditional wheats results in more tillers (extra stems), a thicker stand, and conditions that favor diseases, especially the rusts. A dilemma thus existed: If the farmer used more than a token amount of fertilizer, he depressed the yield through lodging and risked greater losses from diseases. But if he did not use more fertilizer, yields remained low and stagnant because of the impoverished soil.

Before World War II, breeders—especially in Argentina, Australia, Brazil, Britain, Canada, France, India, Italy, Kenya,

Lodging in a tall, weak-stemmed wheat variety. (*Source:* CIMMYT.)

Rhodesia, the United States, and the USSR — had already been working to improve tall spring wheats, primarily by improving stem strength. Nevertheless no developing country had succeeded in raising its national wheat yield above 1250 kg/ha, except Egypt, where the Nile River supplied both fertile soil and irrigation water. Wheat breeders had not yet found the genes that would create plants with strong stems and also with the genetic potential to benefit from increased nutrients.

But the early breeders did identify sources for other improvements in the land races (primitive varietal groupings) bearing names like Gaza (a dryland durum wheat carried to Australia from Palestine by a soldier in World War I) and Turkey (a land race from southern Russia, carried to the United States by Mennonite immigrants in 1877). Progress was made in raising resistance to stem rust and smut and in strengthening winterhardiness.

Oversimplified, that was the breeding situation until World War II. In the postwar period, when Norin 10 dwarfing genes were brought to the Western Hemisphere, they, combined with the genes accumulated in the improved land races, paved the way for the creation of short, lodging-resistant, higher-yielding wheat varieties.

Japanese dwarfs

Japan has had a long history in the development of wheats with reduced height. In 1873 a U.S. agricultural adviser serving the Meiji government wrote a report, which, briefly paraphrased, said: The Japanese have made the dwarfing of wheat an art. The wheat stalk seldom grows longer than 50 to 60 centimeters. The head is short but heavy. No matter how much manure is used, the plant will not grow taller; rather the length of the wheat head is increased. Even on the richest soils, the wheat plants never fall down.

One of the Japanese dwarfs, named Daruma, had the capacity to transfer its short stature to the offspring of other wheats it was crossed with. Daruma was used extensively by Japanese breeders who were seeking higher yields, and one of the crosses made history. First, in 1917 the breeders combined Daruma with Fultz, a land race imported to Japan from the United States, whose origin was believed to be somewhere in the Mediterranean region. Then, in 1925 the breeders combined Daruma-Fultz with Turkey, a Russian land race (via the United States). From this combination came a new Japanese variety, Norin 10, which was released in 1935. Norin 10 had a height of only 52 to 55 centimeters when grown in Japan and was exceptionally high yielding.

The movement of Norin 10 seeds from Japan to the United States and then to Mexico became steps in the story of modern wheat. In 1946 a U.S. agricultural officer serving in Japan saw Norin 10 growing on a research station. Seeds were sent to the United States and distributed to plant scientists. At Washington State University, breeders began making extensive crosses, but for 6 years the offspring were mostly sterile. Then a promising line emerged, designated Norin 10-Brevor, which was further crossed to three U.S. wheats to pick up additional disease resistance. From these crosses came the first semi-dwarf winter-habit variety, Gaines, which was released in 1961. This variety spread rapidly throughout the northwest United States and was used to establish the world record yield for a single wheat crop, 14,100 kg/ha (see Chapter 1).

A tall (125 cm.) variety, left, contrasts with three semi-dwarf varieties released in Mexico. The shortest is 75 centimeters high. (*Source:* CIMMYT.)

In 1953 when Washington State University had a very small amount of early-generation seeds of Norin 10-Brevor, it sent some to breeders in Mexico. The breeders there attempted to transfer Norin 10 genes into spring-habit wheats with good commercial plant types, but the breeders encountered sterility, shriveled grain, and extreme susceptibility to stem rust. After 7 years of trials, despite frequent failure, the first Mexican semi-dwarfs, Pitic 62 and Penjamo 62, were released.

In the following 20 years, a succession of Mexican semi-dwarfs carrying Norin 10 genes swept across the spring-wheat areas of the developing world and large areas of industrialized countries as well. Semi-dwarfs now make up over 50 percent of the spring-wheat crop in developing countries.

Characteristics of semi-dwarf wheats

Some of the characteristics of the new short wheats are attributable to Norin 10 genes and some to careful selection for desirable characteristics from other parent varieties.

• *Short stature.* The height of semi-dwarfs ranges from 50 to 100 centimeters in Mexico compared with 125 to 150 centimeters for the tall traditional varieties.

• *Sturdy straw and strong crown roots.* Semi-dwarfs are resistant to lodging because, in addition to their short height, they have been bred to have sturdy stems, which are less likely to bend or snap, and strong crown roots, which firmly anchor the plant in the soil. Lodging resistance is crucial when high rates of nitrogen fertilizer are applied — which encourages the growth of full, weighty heads — and when high winds or heavy rains strike.

• *More fertile florets.* The new semi-dwarfs can produce 120 to 150 fertile flowers (grains) per head under good management, which gives a high-yield potential when semi-dwarfs are properly spaced and adequately fertilized and watered. The old tall varieties have the potential to produce 50 to 65 grains per head.

• *Higher tillering.* Plants of most semi-dwarf varieties are able to produce 25 to 100 tillers (stems) each. Since each tiller can produce a head of grain, high tillering raises the yield potential. High tillering also is advantageous when poor germination of seed or an inadequate seeding rate causes a sparse stand. High-tillering plants will, to a degree, spread out to close the gaps.

• *Earliness.* Semi-dwarf spring wheats have been selected to reach maturity days or even weeks sooner than the tall wheats. Earliness is important to farmers in areas where the growing season is limited by the rainfall pattern or frost, and to farmers who grow a sequence of crops on the same land in the same year.

• *Fertilizer response.* If moisture is adequate, semi-dwarfs commonly produce 15 to 20 kilograms, and sometimes even 30 kilograms, of additional grain for each kilogram of added nitrogen fertilizer, up to the first 50 to 70 kg/ha of nitrogen. By contrast the old tall wheats produce only 8 to 12 kilograms of additional grain for each added kilogram of nutrients up to the first 50 to 70 kg/ha

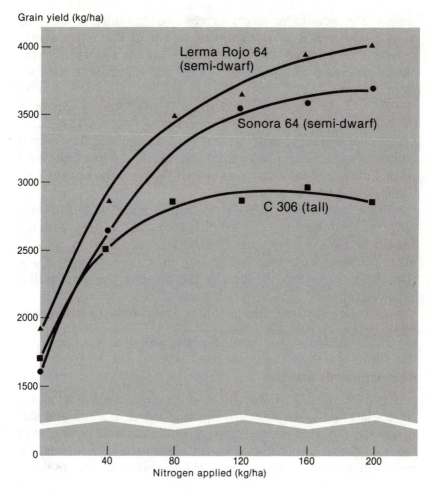

Figure 3. Response to fertilizer of two short varieties and one tall variety of wheat in India, 1965–1966 (avg. of ten trials). (*Source:* Bill C. Wright, 1972. Critical requirements of new dwarf wheat for maximum production. In *Proceedings of the Second FAO/Rockefeller Foundation International Seminar on Wheat Improvement and Production, March 1968.* Beirut: Ford Foundation.)

of nitrogen. Above that level of nitrogen, yields of the tall varieties increase little or not at all because of lodging. Fertilizer response varies somewhat from location to location; Figure 3 shows data from India in 1965–1966.

• *Higher harvest index.* The grain of the best semi-dwarfs receives about half of the carbohydrate the plant produces; the grain of the older taller varieties receives only a third or less. The ratio of the weight of the grain to weight of the entire above-ground plant is called the "harvest index" and is a measure of the plant's efficiency in using light, water, and nutrients to produce grain.

• *Day-length insensitivity.* Many semi-dwarf spring wheats in the Mexican program have been selected to flower and produce grain under a wide range of day lengths. Consequently they are not limited to one latitude or to a fixed planting date. Most traditional wheats are genetically programmed to flower only when a particular length of day occurs.

• *Wide adaptation.* Many semi-dwarfs adjust well to a wide range of temperatures, day lengths, moisture regimes, and soil conditions. Wide adaptation can be transferred genetically to other breeding materials, but testing in a broad range of environments is required to identify the progeny that possess this characteristic.

• *Disease resistance.* Breeders have incorporated resistance to many diseases in the semi-dwarfs.

New agronomic practices

To exploit the full yield potential of the modern wheat plant, the farmer has to modify his management practices: method and date of sowing, moisture management, fertilizer application, and weed control. If the farmer uses old methods on the new wheats, the yield will be little improved over the tall wheats. Moreover the switch to semi-dwarf varieties may even result in a yield reduction if weeds are a serious problem. Therefore agronomic trials are needed to determine which production practices are appropriate for local climates and soils. Agronomic trials are needed in each country, for each soil type, and in each climatic zone.

An illustration of the kinds of information that agronomists should seek before introducing a new wheat variety can be derived from the changes in recommended production practices made in the mid-1960s for the irrigated northern plains of India:

Date of planting
Old way: Plants should emerge by the end of October
New way: Longer-season dwarfs (such as the variety Kalyansona)

are seeded November 1–15, and shorter-season dwarfs (such as Sonalika) are seeded November 15–30.

Depth of seeding
Old way: 10 to 15 centimeters deep
New way: 5 centimeters deep (If seeds for dwarfs are placed more than 5 centimeters deep, many seedlings fail to emerge.)

First two irrigations
Old way: Irrigate before seeding, then again 30 to 35 days after emergence.
New way: Irrigate before seeding, then again about 21 days after emergence when crown roots are forming. (If irrigation is delayed beyond 30 days, the harvest may be reduced by 500 kg/ha, because crown roots cannot establish themselves effectively in dry soil, which results in poor tillering.)

Fertilizer
Old way: 0-0-0 or 56-0-0
New way: 120-60-0

The generalized fertilizer formula for the plains of northern India had to be modified by individual farmers to fit their soil situations and cropping patterns. For example, wheat following cotton will respond more economically to higher levels of fertilization than wheat following legumes.

Disease control

Pliny, the Roman author, wrote in the first century A.D., "The rust of wheat is the greatest pest of crops," and that statement is still accurate. Three rusts—stem, leaf, and stripe—are the most prevalent diseases of wheat and the most destructive. For example, wheat farmers in the United States suffered spectacular losses because of epidemics of stem rust in 1916, 1935, and 1952–1954; of leaf rust in 1938, 1941, 1949, and 1954; and of stripe rust in the Pacific Northwest in 1960–1961. Mexico experienced three consecutive devastating epidemics of stem rust from 1939 to 1941 and a severe epidemic of leaf rust in 1976–1977. Brazil experienced classic epidemics of both stem and leaf rust in the early 1970s, and India had repeated epidemics of all three rusts up to 1950. The worst epidemics of stripe rust are in southern Europe. In Africa, although the East African highlands contain "hot spots" for stem and stripe rust, the continent as a whole has no vast contiguous wheat areas such as those that facilitate epidemics in other parts of the world.

It is significant that stem rust epidemics have not recurred in North America and Mexico in more than a quarter century. This recent freedom from stem rust can be attributed to the widespread planting of varieties that have a broad spectrum of rust resistance, particularly in the southern United States and Mexico where wheat grown during the winter would otherwise provide the pathogen an opportunity to multiply to epidemic proportions.

The three rusts are caused by fungi. Spores spread by the wind travel a few kilometers, then multiply. Occasionally, however, a windborne journey may extend over 3000 kilometers as the spores can be carried by high-altitude winds and, still viable, fall back to earth in raindrops.

When spores land on a susceptible wheat variety and encounter favorable moisture and temperature conditions, they germinate and penetrate the stem, leaf, or head of the plant where they cause pustules (blisterlike swellings), which become little factories for multiplying spores. A reproduction cycle is completed every 10 to 15 days, so trillions of additional spores can be circulating within a month. The released spores spread rapidly from plant to plant of susceptible varieties, and under favorable temperature and moisture conditions, an epidemic develops. Pustules rupture the plant surface, interfere with the plant's reception of sunlight and with its manufacture of plant food, and cause loss of moisture. The plant's growth is slowed, and in extreme circumstances, the plant dies. The pustules of stem rust are typically dark brown (turning black on dying plants). Those of leaf rust are light brown, and those of stripe rust are yellow.

Through evolution, a few wheat land races have developed resistance to some strains of rust, but this defense mechanism is generally narrow in character. That is, one gene in a wheat plant protects against one race of rust. Breeders are striving to achieve broad, stable resistance to rusts, but the task is difficult. First, there are many races of rust (types of spores). They are similar in appearance but differ in their ability to attack different wheat varieties. Second, the races are constantly changing through mutation and sexual mating. Third, the spores of each new race can multiply rapidly and be disseminated long distances by the wind. A world survey of rust pathogens in 1967 identified more than 300 races of stem rust, 189 of leaf rust, and 57 of stripe rust. Others have since been added to the list, and many hundreds of undescribed races no doubt exist.

One way to achieve a broad spectrum of resistance is to incorporate many resistance genes into a wheat variety, and intercrossing varieties that carry different kinds of resistance has been the strategy of most plant breeders. In recent decades, resistance to stem rust has been stabilized, and resistance to stripe rust has been substantially improved, but progress toward a stable resistance to leaf rust has been slower, probably because the pathogen of leaf rust changes more rapidly than the pathogens that cause stem rust and stripe rust.

Chemicals to counter rust have been tested, but the results have not been sufficiently economic to encourage worldwide usage. However, Mexico did use aerial spraying to stop a leaf rust outbreak in 1976–1977, and chemical sprays are used to some extent in Germany, Denmark, and the United States.

Agronomic practices can reduce the dangers of rust. Planting dates can be adjusted or early maturing varieties can be planted, so that the grain ripens before the occurrence of seasonal climatic conditions that encourage rust epidemics to develop. Destroying the rust's alternate host plants will also reduce outbreaks. Alternate hosts are plants other than wheat on which rusts can survive. On such plants, the rust can in time develop new genetic combinations of virulence until new races emerge that have the ability to attack varieties that were previously resistant. No agronomic approach has proved a complete safeguard for long.

In the 1960s, India developed an "early warning system" for identifying new races of rust that have the potential to render previously resistant varieties of wheat susceptible. This warning system has now been extended by international agencies across southern Asia and northern Africa. But a warning is of value only if the country threatened has ready for release new varieties that are resistant to the new races. The country must also be capable of multiplying seed rapidly for distribution to farmers. (Other options for the control of rusts, such as multilines and varietal mixtures, are discussed in Chapter 9.)

The diseases of wheat may someday be controlled as completely as some communicable diseases of the human population (smallpox, for example), but victory over the three rusts appears to be at least several decades in the future, and the victory may never be complete because of the changeability of the fungi. Even if the rusts are conquered, there are many other diseases that cause economic losses, so there is no single or simple solution to the complex problem of the wheat diseases that take a toll of the harvest every year and that have the potential to periodically cause disastrous regional epidemics.

The social impact of modern wheats

In the late 1960s, the modern wheats received a bad rating from some social scientists who had studied the impact of high-yielding varieties of both wheat and rice. They concluded that the so-called green revolution had been a failure because it caused rich farmers to get richer and poor farmers to get poorer. These preliminary findings stimulated hundreds of additional studies in the 1970s, most of which reached contrary conclusions. In 1979 the World Bank employed a consultant, Grant Scobie, to survey this body of literature. The survey covered 529 studies (mostly books and journal articles, all in English) and paid greater attention to the economic literature than to sociology, anthropology, and public administration. Six generalizations can be drawn from this "state of knowledge" report.

• *Neither farm size nor land tenure was a major impediment in the adoption of new cereal varieties.* Larger farmers with better access to information and a greater willingness to bear risks were the first adopters, but within relatively few years, the lags in adoption associated with farm size and land tenure disappeared. The new technology was inherently scale neutral.

• *The new varieties increased the demand for direct agricultural labor per crop and per hectare.* In India one study of wheat and rice found that an average increase of 23 man-days per hectare per crop was needed to cope with increased fertilizer applications and irrigation, better weed control, and greater harvest volume. Assuming an increase of only 10 to 15 man-days of labor for a wheat crop (because wheat is less labor intensive than rice), the 30 million hectares of modern wheats grown in developing countries would require from 300 million to 450 million man-days of additional labor per year, thus benefiting the employment of adopting countries.

The new varieties created secondary employment: for transport, storage, and milling of the crops and for the manufacturing and merchandising of fertilizers, herbicides, and farm tools. Multiple cropping was stimulated by early maturing wheats and the use of fertilizer, which also provided more employment. In India about 30 percent of the increased income from grain crops is spent on other agricultural commodities such as fruits, vegetables, and livestock products, which are more labor intensive than grain production. The balance of the increased income goes for textiles, footwear, and household furniture, again adding to employment.

• *The income of large and small farmers from the new wheats and rice went up by approximately the same proportion.* In West Bengal, India, for example, farmers with less than 1 hectare gained 24 percent in income, and the largest farmers (with 4 to 6 hectares) gained 18 percent in income. There was variation between countries. The absolute gain, as contrasted with the percentage increase, favored the larger farmers, but the small farmers gained proportionally.

• *Low-income consumers were the greatest beneficiaries from the new cereal varieties.* This consequence went almost unnoticed during the first decade. Increased food output tends to depress prices, and since lower-income consumers spend a higher proportion of their total income on food, typically 50 to 80 percent, any decline in food prices confers a disproportionate benefit on them. In Colombia, following the introduction of semi-dwarf rice varieties, the lowest-income earners, those who received only 4 percent of the total family income in the country, captured 28 percent of the economic benefits from the drop in rice prices.

• *The nutritional impact of the new wheats was beneficial.* At the beginning of the revolution, critics in India observed that the new wheats had encroached on land previously planted to pulses and other crops of high nutritional value, and the conclusion was drawn that the increased planting of cereals was harmful to the national diet. But later studies showed that the actual production of calories, protein, and essential amino acids in India was higher in 1975–1976 than it would have been if the new cereals had not been planted. Even though 20 percent of the expansion of the wheat area in six Indian states came at the expense of pulses (low-yielding crops), the enhanced productivity of the new wheats led to a rise in total protein and energy supplies of at least 20 percent. The earlier maturity of some new wheats made multiple cropping possible, which added to the nutritional benefits.

• *The high-yielding varieties increased differences of income between regions within a country.* The new cereal varieties gave greatest initial response in good soils that had adequate fertility and adequate moisture. They did less well in problem soils (acid, saline, poorly drained) and in low-rainfall regions in the absence of irrigation. Some new wheat lines in breeders' plots now combine a higher yield potential with an increased tolerance to acidity and other soil problems. But technology alone will not solve the problems of impoverished agricultural areas. Part of the remedy must be found in increased government investments and services in disadvantaged regions.

In summary, the consensus of the literature is that the management-responsive cereals had an overall beneficial effect upon employment, nutrition, and income distribution. And obviously the increased wheat production saved hundreds of millions of dollars for countries like India, Pakistan, and Turkey, which otherwise would have had to spend the money for food imports to sustain their large and growing populations.

As time passes, the impact of new cereal technology spreads like ripples from a stone cast in the water. Farmers who apply fertilizer to one crop extend the practice to other crops. The changes continue.

Mexico: A Pioneer

During the first half of this century, Mexico's food production was stagnant. The country was importing half its wheat and 20 percent of its total cereal needs by the end of World War II. But during the three decades following the war, many changes occurred. Mexico now produces 2.5 million tons of wheat a year, which makes wheat the third most important cereal crop after maize (10 million tons a year) and sorghum (4 million tons, used almost exclusively for animal feed). Mexico's wheat yield was 4100 kg/ha in 1980, the highest among the developing countries, and with favorable weather, a few farmers harvested 7000 to 8000 kg/ha.

The postwar wheat situation

Wheat was introduced into Mexico by the Spaniards in the seventeenth century, shortly after the conquest. Spanish land races, which were tall, had weak stems, and were susceptible to the major rusts, covered most of the half million hectares of wheat grown in 1945. In years when weather conditions favored the development of stem rust — as in 1939, 1940, and 1941 in the State of Sonora and in 1948 in the Bajio region (see Figure 4), epidemics brought ruin to the wheat farmer. Mexican wheats were then, as now, of spring growth habit, mostly irrigated, planted from October to December and harvested from April to June. Cultural practices followed traditional methods: Oxen and mules were used to pull the wooden plows, harvesting was generally by hand sickle, threshing was done by the trampling of animals, and grain was cleaned by hand winnowing. Soils were poor, and fertilizers almost unknown. In 1945 the average yield of wheat in Mexico was 750 kg/ha; a few of the best Sonora farmers produced 2000 kg/ha under irrigation when the weather was exceptionally favorable,

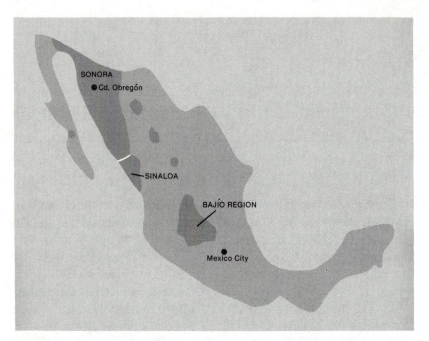

Figure 4. Mexico's wheat-growing areas. The principal areas are the states of Sonora and Sinaloa in the northwest, 600,000 hectares of irrigated wheat; the Bajío, part of the central plateau, 100,000 hectares of irrigated wheat; and scattered small valleys of the central plateau, 60,000 hectares.

and the highest yields on the experiment station were between 3000 and 4000 kg/ha.

Little wheat research had been done in Mexico. The country had only one qualified wheat scientist in 1943 when a research effort on maize, beans, and wheat — the basic food crops — was launched by the Ministry of Agriculture and the Rockefeller Foundation. About 20 years later, two organizations evolved from that collaboration: INIA (the National Institute of Agricultural Research), to serve Mexican agriculture, and CIMMYT (International Maize and Wheat Improvement Center), to serve developing nations (see Appendix).

The research program

At the start, Mexico's wheat program was assigned a few hectares of government land at Chapingo, an agricultural college near

Mexico City. A larger piece of land for wheat research was located in the State of Sonora, 1500 kilometers north of Mexico City. Wheat testing was also conducted at seven other widely dispersed locations. The contrasting environments of the Chapingo station on the rainfed central plateau and the Sonora station on the irrigated northern coastal plain ultimately proved important to the success of Mexican wheats worldwide, but the advantage of the sites was not initially recognized.

Mexico had no large collection of wheat varieties to be used for research. Mixtures of Spanish wheats, gathered from Mexican farmers in 1944, were found to be poor yielding and susceptible to disease. The search for breeding materials turned to other countries. During the first year of testing, Mexico's "seed bank" consisted of 38 entries, including 1 or 2 from the dozen or so countries thought to be the leaders in research on spring bread wheats. Resistance to stem rust, which was considered the most urgent need for wheat growers in Mexico, was the first criterion in assembling the breeding collection.

Conventional breeding procedures in the 1940s required 10 to 12 years to produce a new wheat variety, usually including seven annual breeding or selection cycles plus 3 to 5 years for testing and seed multiplication. The impatient young wheat team in Mexico adopted two shortcuts, both involving calculated risks. First, they identified four imported wheat varieties that they thought might serve Mexico's immediate needs, and in 1946, after 1 year of testing, they released them to farmers. The releases were Kenya 324 and Kenya 321 from East Africa and Supremo 211 and Frontera 209 from the United States. These were not high-yielding varieties compared with later releases, but they showed good resistance to stem rust, and their yield was an improvement over local wheats.

Second, and even more unorthodox, the wheat scientists began to breed or select new varieties of wheat on a schedule of two cycles a year. The winter cycle, November–April, took place in Sonora, which is at 28 degrees north and near sea level. The summer cycle, May–October, took place at Chapingo, which is at 18 degrees north and 2200 meters elevation. The speedup permitted five wheat varieties to be released in 1948 from crosses made in 1945. That was about 7 years faster than the conventional time table.

Table 3
Some spring bread-wheat varieties released in Mexico[a]

Year of release	Variety	Yield potential (kg/ha)	Plant height (cm)	Grain color	Days to maturity	Test weight (kg/hl)	Dwarfing gene[b]
1950	Yaqui 50	4,000	115	Red	138	78.8	–
1960	Nainari 60	4,500	110	Red	138	72.2	–
1962	Pitic 62	5,870	105	Red	140	73.4	Rht2
1962	Penjamo 62	5,870	100	Red	137	78.7	Rht1
1964	Sonora 64	5,580	85	Red	122	79.2	Rht2
1964	Lerma Rojo 64	6,000	100	Red	139	79.8	Rht1
1966	INIA 66	7,000	100	Red	130	82.0	Rht1
1966	Siete Cerros 66	7,000	100	Amber	138	81.5	Rht1
1970	Yecora 70	7,500	75	Amber	138	80.6	Rht1-2
1971	Cajeme 71	7,000	75	Red	140	80.2	Rht1-2
1971	Tanori 71	7,000	90	Red	130	82.8	Rht1
1973	Jupateco 73	7,500	95	Red	128	80.2	Rht1
1973	Torim 73	7,000	75	Amber	130	81.4	Rht1-2
1975	Zaragoza 75	7,500[c]	100	Red	142	79.6	Rht1
1976	Nacozari 76	7,500[c]	90	Amber	138	80.2	Rht1
1976	Pavon 76	7,500[c]	100	Amber	140	82.3	Rht2
1979	CIANO 79	7,500[c]	90	Red	140	80.4	Rht2

[a]Data from irrigated experiment-station plots in the State of Sonora, Mexico, under high soil fertility and essentially disease-free conditions.

[b]Dwarfing genes from Norin 10 variety are abbreviated: Rht1 = reduced height gene 1; Rht2 = reduced height gene 2; Rht1-2 = combined reduced height genes 1 and 2.

[c]Yields during 1975–1979 fluctuated between 7,500 and 9,500 kg/ha because of weather, but a conservative minimum of 7,500 kg/ha is given here.

Between 1948 and 1960, the Mexican program bred and released 20 wheat varieties. They all were tall and somewhat higher yielding, earlier maturing, and more disease resistant, especially to stem rust, than the older varieties. These tall wheats were good enough, when combined with improved cultural practices, to double Mexico's national wheat yield to 1700 kg/ha by 1961, and, in the process, Mexico temporarily became self-sufficient in wheat.

Dwarfing genes

The new Mexican wheats had one serious drawback: They lodged, or fell over, when well fertilized. The highest yielding of them, Nainari 60, rarely exceeded 4500 kg/ha, even when carefully

Table 4
Some durum varieties released in Mexico[a]

Year of release	Variety	Yield potential (kg/ha)	Plant height (cm)	Days to flowering	Test weight (kg/hl)	Pigment[b] (ppm)
1960	Tehuacan 60	4,200	150	100	81	5.5
1965	Oviachic 65	7,000	90	106	81	7.2
1967	Chapala 67	7,000	85	84	83	4.0
1969	Jori C69	7,700	85	83	81	3.7
1971	Cocorit 71	8,300	85	79	81	3.6
1975	Mexicali 75	8,600	90	76	80	5.8
1979	Yavaros C79	8,600	90	84	83	5.0

[a]Measured at experiment station in State of Sonora, under good agronomic practices.

[b]Carotenoid (yellow pigment).

tended on the research station. Lodging discouraged application of more than 50 to 70 kg/ha of nitrogen. After many unsuccessful attempts, a remedy for lodging was found in the Norin 10 dwarfing genes (see Chapter 2). Norin genes not only shortened the plant, but resulted in higher tillering, more grains per head, more grains per square meter, a more efficient use of fertilizer and moisture, and a higher harvest index.

Between 1960 and 1980, Mexico released 39 spring bread-wheat varieties, and some of the more prominent ones are listed in Table 3. Starting with Pitic 62 and Penjamo 62 (the number in each varietal name indicates the approximate year of release), all contained Norin 10 genes.

Durum wheats were also dwarfed. Breeders crossed bread wheats containing Norin 10 genes with durums, and subsequently backcrossed the progeny to durums, which resulted in high-yielding durum varieties. Semi-dwarf durums were released in Mexico (see Table 4) and are now widely grown in durum areas of the developing world. Durum yields benefited even more than bread wheats from dwarfing, because the old durums were taller, had weaker stems, and were lower yielding than the bread wheats. Now the best durum varieties stand up well under heavy fertilization, and their yields equal or surpass those of the best bread wheats.

The release of semi-dwarf wheats broke the Mexican yield bar-

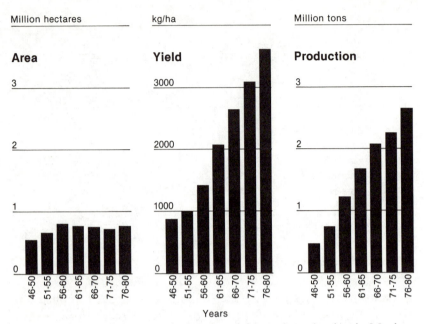

Figure 5. Annual average wheat area, yield, and production in Mexico, 5-year periods, 1946–1980.

rier of 4500 kg/ha. Some farmers in Sonora began to harvest up to 8000 kg/ha from fields as large as 100 hectares, and the national wheat yield rose from 1700 kg/ha in 1961 to 3000 kg/ha in 1970 to 4100 kg/ha in 1980. Figure 5 portrays the changes in Mexican wheat production since 1946.

Response of farmers

The rapid climb of wheat yields in Mexico suggests that farmers were eager for new technology, but they initially were not. Farmers were hostile to the wheats released in the 1940s and to the use of fertilizer. They showed no confidence in scientists, who were perceived as impractical academicians, and adoption of new varieties was slow for the first 5 years.

When the first field day for wheat was organized in 1948 by the research station in the State of Sonora, no more than 25 persons attended despite widespread publicity. And only 5 of that audience were actually farmers, the rest were government officials. By 1951, however, many farmers had gained confidence in the varieties and respect for the scientists. Attendance at annual field days then rose rapidly to 200 to 400 to 800 to 2000 to 4000 in successive years.

Farmers nevertheless were slow to use fertilizers. Supplies were scarce, and many farmers considered fertilizer a risky investment.

Seed multiplication

Seeds of the semi-dwarf wheats were distributed promptly to Mexican farmers, but not by the methods familiar to most governments. Instead research scientists initially took charge of multiplying seeds, and the seeds were spread from farmer to farmer.

Phenomenal speed was demonstrated in multiplying seed for one of the first semi-dwarfs, Sonora 64. Two hundred grams of seed (literally a handful) were increased to 100 tons of seed in 1 year by using adequate fertilizer, water, sparse seeding, and care. The first 200 grams were sown in northwest Mexico on October 5, 1963, and yielded 22 kilograms in February 1964. The plot was cut partially green, and the grain was force-dried. Three kilograms were set aside for research, and the remaining 19 kilograms were seeded at the rate of 8 kg/ha in the first days of March 1964, still in northwest Mexico. A harvest of 3800 kilograms was cut on June 15. The seeds were immediately transported to the Bajio, a highland region, where 3500 kilograms were seeded on June 18 at the conventional rate of 100 kg/ha. From the 35-hectare field, 100,000 kilograms were harvested in October 1964 in good time for the regular winter sowing by farmers in the State of Sonora.

There are lessons here. Seed supply is often a bottleneck in transferring technology from the research station to farmers' fields. The multiplication of Sonora 64 shows what can be done under pressure to introduce a new variety: The multiplication was 500,000 to 1 in 12 months, and it was accomplished by the research staff, with the cooperation of farmers, but in the absence of a government seed agency. Despite demonstrations like this, ineffective seed programs remain a common obstacle to the spread of new wheats.

New agronomy

As new varieties and fertilization were introduced, researchers simultaneously worked on other aspects of crop management, which would have to change in order to maximize the benefits. In the 1950s and 1960s, researchers had to study dates of planting for the new wheats, seeding rate, depth of seed placement, weed control, and irrigation methods to develop new combinations of production practices that would make more efficient use of fertilizers.

Weeds caused wheat little difficulty in infertile soils, but when fertilizer was applied, weeds became a critical problem. Control measures were needed to keep weeds from competing with wheat for nutrients and water.

Wheat in Mexico had no serious insect enemies before these changes began, but after the introduction of high-tillering varieties and fertilizers, certain insects found the dense stands of wheat a favorable environment for multiplication. The English grain aphid, for example, which had never been of economic importance before, occasionally multiplied rapidly and caused severe losses when climatic conditions reduced the population of predators. It was necessary to find a suitable insecticide and develop a method of application for aphid control when predators were inadequate, generally once every 5 or 6 years.

Low soil fertility was initially the most serious limitation on wheat production in the highlands. In trials in the old soils of central Mexico, some unfertilized check plots yielded less than 200 kg/ha. The best-fertilized plots in the same soils yielded 4000 kg/ha for the tall wheats and 7000 kg/ha or more for the semi-dwarfs.

Only nitrogen fertilizer gave economic response in the early years. Phosphorus response in central Mexico became widespread about 4 years after nitrogen fertilization was introduced. The rich coastal soils of Sonora, however, did not begin to respond to phosphorus until 10 years after the introduction of nitrogen fertilizers. Wheat in Mexico does not yet respond to applications of potassium or micronutrients, but at some future date it will. Fertilizer trials in farmers' fields must be a continuing undertaking.

Fertilizer recommendations for wheat have evolved as varieties have changed and farming practices have intensified. The first recommendation for tall wheats in 1950 was 40-0-0 or 40-40-0 (kilograms of nutrient nitrogen, phosphorus, and potassium per hectare). Ten years later, the recommendation for tall wheats was up to 80-40-0. When semi-dwarfs became available, the recommendation rose to 120-40-0, and still later to 140-40-0, where it remained at the beginning of the 1980s. Some farmers in Sonora exceed the recommendations, applying 200 kg/ha of nitrogen to semi-dwarfs. The crop that precedes wheat can modify these requirements. For example, 160-40-0 may be needed for wheat after cotton, whereas 120-40-0 may be sufficient after soybeans.

Rust resistance

A broad spectrum of disease resistance contributed to the success of the Mexican semi-dwarf wheats. Despite continuing changes in the races of the three major rusts, Mexico has had only one severe epidemic since 1951, and that was leaf rust. Mexico monitors the reactions to rusts of varieties in farmers' fields. As virulent new races of rust organisms cause commercial varieties to become susceptible, new resistant varieties are quickly released. The rapidly changing pattern of leaf rust races limits the useful life of most Mexican varieties to fewer than 5 years. To keep pace, about half the wheat researchers in Mexico focus on disease-related work, which slows research on other subjects.

Leaf rust epidemic, 1976–1977

An epidemic of leaf rust occurred in the northwestern states of Sinaloa and Sonora in the 1976–1977 season, providing new lessons in rust control. There had been little loss in this region to rusts for 25 years because of the widespread use of resistant varieties. A generation of farmers and government researchers had grown up who had never experienced an epidemic, and they were complacent about the danger.

Leaf rust is endemic in Mexico's northwestern states where more than 70 percent of the nation's wheat crop is produced on 600,000 hectares of irrigated land. Leaf rust may cause an 80 to 100 percent loss of yield when young plants of a susceptible variety are attacked. But in most years, the first symptoms of leaf rust appear in early March, and the peak of infection is reached 1 month later when the plants are approaching maturity. Consequently losses are usually only 5 to 10 percent.

The 1977 epidemic was preceded by clear warnings 2 years earlier. Monitoring trials in 1975 showed that half the races of leaf rust in Mexico were capable of attacking Jupateco 73, the most widely grown variety of bread wheat. Normal precautions had been taken: Four previously released varieties of bread wheat retained their resistance to leaf rust, and three new varieties with different sources of rust resistance were released in 1976. But several developments interfered with the routine switch by farmers to the resistant varieties.

During the winter of 1975–1976, landless workers invaded the land of some wheat growers, creating confusion over future ownership and uncertainty whether crops — soybeans and sesame in the summer and wheat in the winter — would be planted in 1976. In addition a shortage of irrigation water in the summer of 1976 reduced the plantings of summer crops. As a result, many farmers left fields of wheat stubble uncultivated during the summer. In July light rains fell, and volunteer wheat seedlings (from seed inadvertently dropped during harvest) of Jupateco 73 emerged. The seedlings were soon infected with leaf rust, and rust spores multiplied. The land tenure problems also discouraged seed organizations from multiplying seed of newly released varieties, so it became difficult for most farmers to buy seed of resistant wheat varieties for planting in 1976.

In October, 2 months before normal planting dates, many farmers took advantage of rains from hurricane Liza and planted a substantial area to Jupateco 73. These plantings were soon infected by spores from the summer volunteer plants. Farmers who waited until December also planted large areas of Jupateco 73, thus providing an opportunity for heavy infection throughout the wheat-growing cycle. Many farmers of the area had never seen an epidemic and did not heed the warnings of scientists to use substitute varieties. By January 1977, there was severe infection in the fields of Jupateco 73 that had been planted ahead of the normal season.

Fortunately the agricultural authorities then took two measures of control. They advised farmers to plow up fields of wheat that had not headed and that had advanced rust and to replant the land to safflower. Fifteen thousand hectares were replaced under this policy. In addition the Ministry of Agriculture sprayed 70,000 hectares of Jupateco 73 by airplane with fungicides, which had been hurriedly imported. This step stopped the epidemic and saved the crop. Fields of Jupateco 73 that were not sprayed produced 700 to 900 kg/ha of unmarketable grain, but some nearby fields that were sprayed properly and at the right time produced superior yields of 5000 to 5500 kg/ha.

Government officials concluded that fungicides can be a successful emergency measure against leaf rust epidemics, at least in the absence of rainfall, which could wash away the chemicals. The fungicides do not eradicate the disease, but they diminish losses. The officials also reaffirmed their belief that the safest and most economical control measure is to ensure that new varieties with different sources of rust resistance are always available for distribution to farmers as rapidly as the older wheat varieties become susceptible to changing rust pathogens.

Private support for agricultural research

A remarkable aspect of the Mexican wheat program is the farmers' organization Patronato para la Investigacíon y Experimentacíon Agricola de Estado de Sonora (Supporters of Agricultural Research in the State of Sonora). This public service organization combines the efforts of 34 bodies such as farmers' cooperative associations, credit banks, marketing boards, and agribusiness agencies.

Patronato has donated 245 hectares of prime agricultural land in Sonora for agricultural research, and it contributes US$900,000 a year for agricultural research. These funds are raised by a voluntary quota levied by the farmers upon their own crop sales. Originally each wheat farmer contributed one quarter percent of the proceeds from the sale of his wheat, but the voluntary contribution has gradually risen to more than 2 percent. The farmers who are members of Patronato produced over half of Mexico's wheat crop during the 1970s. Few countries have been served so well by a multipurpose agricultural organization, but countries like Mexico, Japan, and South Korea that have efficient service organizations have achieved extraordinary agricultural growth.

Training scientists

A skilled Mexican scientific staff grew up with the research program. From 1945 to 1960, before semi-dwarf wheats appeared on Mexican farms, 750 young Mexican university graduates gained experience in the research fields and laboratories. Those students who demonstrated an aptitude and a motivation for research or extension won fellowships to go abroad to study toward advanced agricultural degrees. Three hundred returned with master's degrees and 100 with doctorates. These young men and women later staffed INIA, the National Institute of Agricultural Research, which was formed in 1960.

In 1959 Mexico initiated its own graduate program in agricultural education, and by 1980 the government was supporting five agricultural universities, which are located in different climatic zones of the country. The fellowship program, which began with foreign aid, was replaced in the late 1960s by CONACYT, the National Council of Science and Technology, which awards hundreds of fellowships each year for advanced study in agriculture and other areas.

It took 20 to 25 years to staff the various Mexican agricultural agencies with sufficient scientists. And the need for training continues partly because experienced scientists move out of government agencies to private corporations that deal with credit, fertilizers, farm machinery, and seed sales, and their places are taken by younger scientists emerging from the universities.

Benefits of wheat research

The wheat research done in Mexico since 1945 was worth, in terms of additional wheat output, US$460 million a year by 1980. But the world as a whole benefited too. Seeds of semi-dwarf wheats were sent out of Mexico, and by 1980 these varieties or their descendants were used to sow half the spring wheat crop in developing countries, thus adding to food production in the 1960s and 1970s.

But the most profound benefits of Mexico's experience are the innovations in wheat research techniques, which have been exported worldwide and are helping many countries increase their food supply. For example, Mexico gathered a working collection of wheat varieties from other countries and eventually screened the world collection of wheats (30,000 entries) for new sources of high yield and disease resistance. All successful wheat programs are now using larger collections of germ plasm than was the practice before World War II, which increases their chances of success in breeding better varieties.

Another innovation is the scale of the crossing program. More wheat crosses have been made in Mexico than in any other country — about 200,000 crosses between 1950 and 1980. This "numbers game" resembles roulette. It is based on the premise that a winning combination of genes will occur rarely and therefore it is necessary to make crosses in volume, and screen the progeny intensively, to

CIMMYT conducts its winter-season wheat research at the CIANO station in the State of Sonora, in Mexico. Most semi-dwarf Mexican wheats were originally crossed at this station, and seed for CIMMYT's worldwide nurseries is multiplied in these fields. (*Source:* CIMMYT.)

find ones that are outstanding. Most developing countries have applied this philosophy by annually testing the international nurseries, which represent a selection of the crosses made by many wheat programs (see Chapter 7).

A third innovation is the practice of growing two generations of progeny from crosses each year, thus reducing by half the time needed to develop a new variety. Many developing countries now follow this practice. Fourth, by testing advanced breeding lines in more than 100 countries, Mexico quickly learns whether the progeny can produce under widely varying temperatures, moisture regimes, and soil conditions and whether they have broad resistance to diseases. Widely adapted lines have three advantages: They reduce the farmer's vulnerability to year-to-year fluctuations in weather and diseases, they simplify seed multiplication and distribution, and they serve many countries. Fifth, early-segregating populations (F_2 generation) are supplied by CIMMYT to developing nations that have trained personnel and research stations suitable for exploiting this material.

Mexico's future wheat imports

Mexico was self-sufficient in wheat from 1956 to 1971, but by the end of the 1970s, Mexico was importing a third of its wheat needs. One reason is that Mexico's population increased more than threefold between 1940 and 1980. In addition, the land suitable for wheat production in the winter season is limited. Furthermore, Mexico has chosen to expand production of export commodities such as fresh fruits, vegetables, and meats, which are labor intensive, to provide more employment. Mexico's current agricultural exports to the United States are worth more than US$2000 million a year, and imports of agricultural products (including wheat and maize) are valued at less than US$1000 million a year, which means the agricultural trade balance is substantially in Mexico's favor.

Mexico may continue to import part of its wheat requirements so long as its farmers can continue to produce export commodities that command higher prices. Mexico's average wheat yields will probably surpass 5000 kg/ha during the 1980s, possibly reaching 5500 or 6000 kg/ha by the end of the century. The Mexican fall-planted wheat crop will also spread into areas not now growing wheat, and more wheat will be grown during the summer in rain-fed areas at higher elevations.

4
India and Pakistan: The Asian Leaders

The arrival of semi-dwarf wheats from Mexico triggered wheat revolutions in India and Pakistan in the 1960s. Both countries approximately doubled their wheat production between 1966 and 1971.

India's wheat program

Semi-dwarf wheats reached India in 1962 with the International Spring Wheat Rust Nursery, a group of varieties made available for worldwide testing by the U.S. Department of Agriculture. When the nursery was grown at Delhi, Indian wheat scientists spotted the Mexican semi-dwarfs Pitic 62 and Penjamo 62 and concluded that, with their strong short stems and good rust resistance, the Indian yield ceiling of 3500 kg/ha might be broken. India at the time was importing more than 2 million tons of wheat annually.

The Mexican varieties were subsequently tested on three Indian research stations in 1962–1963 and performed well. Norman Borlaug visited India in 1963, at government invitation, and arranged to supply 100 kilograms of each of four short wheat varieties from Mexico and small samples of about 600 advanced lines. In trials harvested in the spring of 1964, two Mexican semi-dwarfs, Sonora 64 and Lerma Rojo 64, outyielded all Indian check varieties by 30 percent.

By 1964 the Indian government had committed itself to a dynamic national wheat production program built around the new semi-dwarfs. The campaign involved a vigorous wheat-testing program on research stations, agronomy trials at numerous sites, a speedup in seed multiplication, a demonstration program in farmers' fields that eventually covered all wheat-producing states, and a mammoth importation of Mexican wheat seed.

Agronomy and variety trials

Comprehensive agronomy trials were designed to investigate depth and method of sowing, planting dates and seeding rates, nitrogen rates with and without phosphorus, timing and method of nitrogen application, optimum date of first irrigation, and critical timing and amounts of irrigation for optimum yield. Two Mexican semi-dwarfs, Sonora 64 and Lerma Rojo 64, were used in the trials.

From these tests came recommendations to farmers on how to grow the new wheats. The agronomists found, for example, that seeds of semi-dwarfs should be planted no more than 5 centimeters deep and that planting dates could be delayed past late October, the usual time for planting traditional Indian wheats. Some semi-dwarfs could be planted as late as November 15, and planting of early maturing semi-dwarfs could be as late as December 1. The

Farmers in India standing on stools to winnow grain. (*Source:* Bill Wright.)

agronomists discovered the importance of irrigating about 21 days after plant emergence, because that is when the crown roots are forming and they will not become well established in dry soil. The agronomists developed fertilizer data that encouraged the application of 120 to 140 kg/ha of nitrogen, replacing the old recommendation of 40 kg/ha. The same trials confirmed the 2-to-1 ratio between nitrogen and phosphorus requirements, hence 60 kg/ha of phosphorus was the initial recommendation. Little or no response to potassium was found except in sandy soils.

Seed increase

Because there was no government agency to multiply wheat seeds in the mid-1960s, IARI (Indian Agricultural Research Institute), which was responsible for the wheat program, had to be innovative. IARI designated a village of progressive farmers near Delhi to serve as a "seed village." Using government seed stocks, this village was expected to produce seed of high quality and sell the output to neighboring villages, assisted by government publicity. The scheme was not sufficiently successful to be expanded, however. Instead responsibility for seed multiplication passed to other organizations. The Punjab Agricultural University at Ludhiana and the Uttar Pradesh Agricultural University at Pantnagar undertook to multiply seed of Sonora 64 and Lerma Rojo 64 and to organize demonstrations nearby. Their success encouraged other agricultural universities to join the effort, and state seed farms also assisted. Before the end of the 1960s, the National Seed Corporation entered the wheat seed business.

First farm demonstrations

A large-scale demonstration of semi-dwarf wheats was organized in 1965, made possible by seed multiplied in India and by a shipment of 250 tons of Sonora 64 and Lerma Rojo 64 from Mexico. Researchers at IARI concentrated their demonstrations on farms near their headquarters in Delhi (see Figure 6), and the two universities in Punjab and Uttar Pradesh laid out trials throughout their states.

The demonstrations were conducted on private farms and consisted of about a quarter hectare grown "Your Way" and a quarter hectare grown "Our Way." The former involved the farmer's seed and his own cultivation practices. The latter used a semi-dwarf

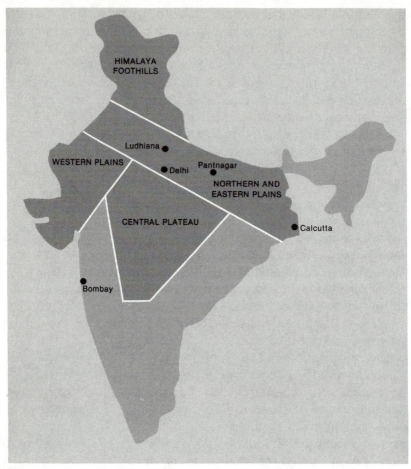

Figure 6. India's wheat-growing areas. About 60 percent of 22 million hectares of wheat are planted in the northern and eastern plains in the states of Punjab, Haryana, Uttar Pradesh, Bihar, and Bengal. Less-extensive wheat areas are in the central plateau, especially in Madhya Pradesh and in the arid western plains, notably Rajasthan. There are scattered wheat areas in the Himalaya foothills.

variety and agronomic practices developed by the research service, including applying 120 kg/ha of nitrogen and 60 kg/ha of phosphorus. Farmers who grew the demonstrations were allowed to keep the seed.

Despite poor germination of the imported seed (probably caused by fumigants improperly applied in Mexico), the wheat harvest in

1966 was greater than in 1965 (12 million tons compared with 11 million tons).

Record seed importation

A record-breaking quantity of seed was imported from Mexico by India in 1966. India had had below normal rains during the 1965–1966 crop season, and the outlook for the monsoon in the summer of 1966 was poor. As a result, the Indian cabinet called for emergency measures to protect the food supply. The minister of agriculture, after reviewing the progress of wheat research, made the daring recommendation that India should import 18,000 tons of wheat seed from Mexico. The cabinet approved.

A seed purchase of this magnitude involves a number of special problems. The Indian government sent a three-man mission to Mexico to safeguard the operation. The mission leader, a high government official, negotiated permission from the Mexican Ministry of Agriculture to purchase wheat standing in farmers' fields, thus bypassing the Mexican seed agency and reducing the price. A second team member examined 10,000 hectares of wheat in 2 weeks and approved the purchase of the crop from 6000 hectares, which had an average yield above 3000 kg/ha. The third member of the mission was responsible for overseeing cleaning, bagging, and shipping of seed from the Mexican port of Guaymas. Here again ingenuity was needed. Fearing that the burlap bags would not withstand loading and unloading, the mission leader had some grain bags dropped 5 meters to a concrete warehouse floor to see whether they would burst. When they did, stronger bag stitching was requested. As a result of these precautions, the shipment arrived in India with almost no loss, and germination in Indian fields averaged 98 percent, an extraordinary accomplishment.

National demonstrations, 1966–1968

With so much imported seed on hand, supplementing local seed, IARI organized a national demonstration program in 1966 in cooperation with the states and universities, involving hundreds of half-hectare plots in farmers' fields. Every research station was given a quota of wheat demonstrations to be planted within its locality. Each plot was modeled on the Your Way and Our Way pattern, which had been pioneered by the research service but was now expanded to include the extension service. In addition seed was distributed by state agencies directly to farmers, giving preference to smallholders, each of whom received 100 kilograms. The entire program involved 150,000 farmers.

In the 1967 harvest, yields were measured on the demonstrations: Your Way averaged 1200 kg/ha, and Our Way gave 2000 to 3000 kg/ha. Much of the semi-dwarf wheat harvested in 1967 was saved for seeding the next crop. The national wheat harvest of 16.5 million tons in 1968, compared with 11.3 million tons in 1967, was the first evidence that a wheat revolution was under way.

Aggressive breeding program

India did not rely long on imported wheat varieties. Indian scientists identified two Mexican advanced lines that performed better than Sonora 64 and Lerma Rojo 64, and by careful selection within each population, Indian scientists developed new varieties that were as disease resistant as any semi-dwarf previously released in Mexico. These two lines were given the names of Kalyansona and Sonalika when released in 1967, and within a few years, they became the most widely grown varieties of spring wheat in the developing world.

Indian breeders then began crossing the best tall Indian wheats with the best Mexican semi-dwarfs. From this work, there emerged a series of new Indian varieties, which are increasingly prominent in the Indian commercial crop—names like Arjun or varietal numbers with the prefix HD, HI, HP, HW, WG, and WL. These varieties carry Norin 10 dwarfing genes from the Mexican side of their parentage, and their yields are comparable to those of Mexican semi-dwarfs.

Competition sometimes played a useful role in these developments. India and Pakistan were watching each other's progress and quietly competing. Rivalry within the various government and university programs in India led to the development of Kalyansona. IARI and the agricultural universities at Ludhiana and Pantnagar had received small quantities of seed of Mexican advanced lines, and all three independently identified the line S227 as the best-adapted semi-dwarf for the Indian environment. All three also selected within that line for improved rust resistance and were rapidly multiplying seed, but they were calling their products by different names—one university used the name Kalyan 227 and the other, Sona 227. The government had to choose which variety to release to farmers, and it decided to compromise. In 1967 the two names were combined to form "Kalyansona." This variety is derived from the Mexican cross number 8156, as are the notable varieties Siete Cerros (white grain) and Super-X (red grain), but by reselection Indian scientists had given the line better disease resistance and had justifiably conferred an Indian name on the result.

The most widely grown Indian wheat variety of the 1970s, Sonalika, has a similar history. Line S308 was bred in Mexico, but because it was susceptible to Mexican races of leaf rust, it was never released to Mexican farmers. After seed samples arrived, Indian scientists made selections for resistance to stem rust and leaf rust, and from this process, Sonalika emerged.

After Sonalika was released in India in 1967, Pakistani farmers obtained seed from Indians along their common border, and it was designated Blue Silver in Pakistan. It is still widely grown. Sonalika covers a large area in India, Pakistan, Nepal, and Bangladesh. Its commercial life of over a dozen years in widespread production without major damage from rust is unequaled. But in the 1980s, Sonalika began to be susceptible to a new race of leaf rust, so it must be replaced.

Pakistan's wheat experience

In 1961 the FAO arranged for young Pakistani wheat scientists to receive practical training in Mexico. On returning home, they brought seed samples of semi-dwarf wheat and considerable knowledge of how the seeds should be grown. In tests on the Pakistani research stations from 1962 to 1964, the semi-dwarfs performed well. On this evidence, Pakistan imported 350 tons of Mexican seed in 1965 and 32,000 tons of seed in 1968. Thus was launched a wheat campaign called the All-Pakistan Wheat Research and Production Program, led by the president of Pakistan, who was himself a landowner and farmer as well as a career army officer.

The Pakistani program had several interesting features.

- Each year from 1963 to 1968, Pakistan sent 5 young wheat scientists to Mexico for experience in research. These 30 scientists subsequently filled key positions in the wheat campaign. This pattern of staff development set a precedent for other national programs.

- "Microplots" were established jointly by the research and extension services in order to select the best wheat varieties. A microplot was a half hectare containing 36 varieties of wheat, both local and Mexican, and such microplots were repeated at more than 50 sites throughout Pakistan. Field days were held at each microplot for farmers in the vicinity.

- When the first semi-dwarf wheat varieties were selected for promotion, the seed increase was accomplished by choosing 1400 outstanding farmers, each of whom multiplied seed for one season and sold the resulting harvest as seed to neighboring farmers.

Wheat production in Pakistan rose from 3.9 million tons in 1966 (the last pre-dwarf year) to 7.3 million tons in 1971, a gain of 90 percent, achieved partly by increased area but largely by increased yields. The national average yield rose from 760 to 1171 kg/ha between 1966 and 1971, and it reached 1500 kg/ha during the late 1970s. The area planted to semi-dwarf wheats expanded steadily. In 1980 the new wheats covered 75 percent or more of Pakistan's wheat land, and the wheat harvest reached 10.8 million tons.

Supporting services for agriculture

The wheat campaigns in India and Pakistan benefited greatly from the existing agricultural services in those countries, such as irrigation systems, toolmaking workshops, fertilizer factories, and agricultural universities. Without these facilities, the wheat revolutions in those countries would not have moved so quickly.

Irrigation

In 1965 India had 26 million hectares of land irrigated by river diversion, and Pakistan had 11 million; this water benefited about 40 percent of the wheat in India and 60 percent in Pakistan. Irrigation networks in both countries included some dams and canals dating from colonial days. Irrigation gave the higher-yielding semi-dwarf wheats a quick start, and profits from growing wheat soon enabled farmers to invest in small wells for irrigation. Called tubewells, they typically lifted groundwater 20 to 40 meters through a narrow pipe (5- to 7.5-centimeter diameter) and were powered by diesel or electric pumps. They delivered enough water for supplemental irrigation on 5 to 10 hectares. Wells were drilled with local labor, and several neighbors often shared a well. Within a decade, Indian farmers had installed 800,000 private wells, and Pakistani farmers 500,000.

These small wells proved more serviceable than the larger, deeper, and more costly government-owned wells, which could not distribute water to their command areas without concrete channels; in addition they were often out of order.

Metal-working shops

As the wheat revolution created a demand for new agricultural implements, ingenious workshops on both sides of the India-Pakistan border developed new products. Combined seed-fertilizer drills and rubber-tired carts, both ox-drawn, became common sights. Then came motors, pumps, and tubing for irrigation wells. Even mechanical wheat threshers were designed and produced locally. Finally, as small tractors spread by the thousands, local machine shops began providing tractor attachments and repair services.

Fertilizer factories

In 1965 India's four nitrogen fertilizer factories had an annual capacity of 160,000 tons of nutrient nitrogen. But within 3 years, the demand of Indian farmers for nitrogen fertilizer outran the supply, and imports expanded rapidly. Nitrogen fertilizer production doubled every 5 years during the 1960s and 1970s, reaching 2 million tons by 1978. Even then, however, India was importing 800,000 tons of nitrogen fertilizer.

Pakistan in 1965 depended largely on imported fertilizer. Within a decade, four large nitrogen factories had been erected, but despite this investment, fertilizer supply could not keep pace with demand.

Agricultural universities

IARI and the excellent network of Indian agricultural universities had turned out hundreds of agricultural graduates by the end of the 1960s and had provided India with a huge supply of trained individuals. The wheat revolution benefited especially from the universities at Ludhiana and Pantnagar, both located in wheat-growing areas. These universities were patterned after the U.S. land-grant universities and blessed with dynamic leaders. They became important participants in the national wheat campaign.

Pakistan was served well by Lyallpur Agricultural University, whose undergraduate college dates back to colonial times. Pakistan also created agricultural colleges at Peshawar and Tando-jam — each serving a different climatic region.

Few developing countries have found themselves so well endowed with agricultural scientists and services when rapid agricultural changes began.

Controversies

Arguments against new technology have been raised in every country where the wheat revolution has altered traditional ways. In India and Pakistan, four issues in particular provoked debate between one group of officials who were satisfied with the status quo and another group who were impatient for progress. These old issues are now settled, but they still carry lessons for countries that are introducing or expanding the use of new wheats.

Grain color

"Our people prefer chapaties made from local white wheat and not the red wheat that comes from abroad" was the argument of some well-fed civil servants and scientists. But though it was true that people preferred chapaties made from the *atta* (whole wheat flour) of white-grained wheats, this preference had not always existed. Until World War I, almost all wheat grown in colonial India had been reddish, and most wheat imported during the 1960s was reddish also. At the height of this controversy, a prominent official in Pakistan required that some of his protesting civil servants take a blindfold test, eating chapaties made from the two colors of wheat, and no one could tell the difference by taste or texture.

Since white and red wheat each have the same nutritional value, policymakers in both India and Pakistan decided to release the reddish grain to farmers immediately. Within a few years, the breeders had succeeded in developing substitute varieties with the preferred white color.

Straw supply

"Short varieties give less *bhoosa*, and therefore our cattle will starve." *Bhoosa* is the Urdu word for the finely chopped cereal straw that is fed to cattle. Careful trials proved that the sparse stands of the old tall wheats, typically grown under low-fertility levels, gave less straw than the new short wheats that were grown with fertilizer in dense stands. The issue disappeared when widespread cultivation of semi-dwarf wheats produced an over-supply of *bhoosa*.

Research versus extension

In some states, the extension service claimed jurisdiction over demonstrations of new wheats to farmers, but their field plots before 1965 were so poorly managed that farmers' production methods were better. Three things were wrong: Researchers had not yet developed new agronomic practices for the short wheats, the extension workers were poorly trained and had inadequate transport for supervising the demonstrations, and there was too little weeding. In 1965 researchers put their short-wheat trials on private farms, which caused friction between research and extension workers. The controversy was settled by the invention of a new classification, the "maximization trial" (maximum yield trial), on which the two services were able to cooperate.

Spreading fertilizer thin

"Considering India's scarce resources, the agronomists' recommendation to apply nitrogen fertilizer on irrigated wheat at 120 kg/ha is wasteful compared with applying 40 kg/ha on each of 3 hectares." This challenge was raised within the Indian Planning Commission. The planners were right in one sense: Fertilizer trials had shown that 120 kilograms of nitrogen will produce more grain if spread over 3 hectares rather than concentrated on 1 hectare. But in another sense, the planners were wrong. When 40 kilograms of nitrogen are applied to 1 hectare, the yield increase is not dramatic compared with the farmer's traditional practice. By contrast, if 120 kilograms of nitrogen are applied to 1 hectare, the farmer who sees the demonstration is impressed by the difference — often three times the yield with no fertilizer — and is more

easily persuaded to try the new practice. The Ministry of
Agriculture, after heated debate, backed the agronomists, and India used fertilizer in its irrigated demonstration plots at the rate of
120-60-0 or 120-60-40.

Second-generation problems

Initial jubilation over the wheat revolution in India was followed by "second-generation problems": seed replacement, grain
storage, support prices, and the impact of wheat upon the cropping pattern.

Seed replacement

By the late 1960s, seed of the two new wheat varieties, Kalyansona and Sonalika, was in great demand. The seed could not be
imported because these varieties, unlike earlier semi-dwarf
varieties, had not been released in Mexico. To fill the need, Uttar
Pradesh Agricultural University developed a service organization,
the Tarai Development Corporation (TDC), which contributed
new methods to seed management. First, TDC used part of the
6400 hectares of university farms to multiply foundation wheat
seed. Then it organized outstanding farmers to grow seed under
TDC contracts and supervision. TDC ensured the quality of the
seed by importing fungicides to treat the seed to control loose
smut, a disease transmitted by infected seed.

The TDC also developed a network of salesmen to deliver seed
to villages. The new seed channels spread semi-dwarf wheats
rapidly into eastern India and into the wheat-growing areas of the
far south. Closer to home, TDC organized agricultural fairs,
which were attended by as many as 20,000 farmers, and sold the
farmers seed packets limited to 1 kilogram, with a postcard re-
questing a report on the results of the seed. Farmers were flattered
to serve as scientific participants, and a large proportion of the
postcards were returned.

Grain storage

India developed a surplus of food grains before the end of the
1960s and began to accumulate buffer stocks. When the first
wheat crop over 16 million tons was harvested in 1968 (5 million
tons more than the year before), India's government and private

storage capacities for all crops totaled only 3 million tons. Some schools and other public buildings were closed, and their rooms were used as temporary grain bins. By 1971 the buffer stocks had reached 11 million tons, and by 1978, 22 million tons. About 9 million tons of the grain reserve was held in good-quality moisture-proof storage, but the rest of the storage was improvised. Some grain was piled on the ground and covered with plastic. Indian officials say grain losses have been low, but they concede that storage is a major problem for those countries that achieve success in a wheat revolution.

The Indian stockpile of grain carried the country through 1979, which had the poorest monsoon rains in 90 years, without wheat or rice imports jamming the ports and without a disastrous drawdown of foreign exchange.

Support prices

Along with buffer stocks came the problem of support prices and an outlay of funds to purchase grain. As soon as wheat production surpasses consumption, farmers must be assured a support price at planting time and a market at harvesttime, or they will reduce the planted area and apply less fertilizer. India had no support prices before the wheat revolution, but it now sets the annual support price before the planting season, generally at or near the world price.

Cropping pattern

The wheat revolution has had a major impact upon India's cropping pattern. Farmers who learned to apply fertilizer on wheat extended the practice to the rest of their crops. Tubewells installed to serve wheat in winter also serve summer crops before the onset of the monsoon rains. Perhaps most important, early-maturing wheat varieties stimulated double cropping and even some triple cropping. For example, Sonalika can be planted about December 1, 30 days later than the tall wheats, and harvested at the traditional time in spring. This possibility allows farmers to have a rice-wheat rotation on large areas in Punjab, Uttar Pradesh, Bihar, and West Bengal where only one crop had been possible before. In West Bengal alone, more than 500,000 hectares of wheat were added in the 1970s, all of it land that is being double cropped for the first time.

Although wheat in a rice-wheat rotation gives lower yields, the total output of grain per hectare per year is greatly increased. There is still a need to develop earlier-maturing rice varieties to facilitate this rotation. A few highly skilled farmers have developed triple-cropping systems such as wheat-beans-rice or wheat-rice-potatoes.

The increase in multiple cropping has promoted mechanization. The climate of much of India allows only 30 days for wheat threshing before the monsoon rains begin. Tight scheduling encourages the use of mechanical wheat threshers, which have appeared by the thousands, mostly manufactured in India.

Some conclusions about India and Pakistan

India's 1979 wheat harvest was 25 million tons greater than the average harvest in the early 1960s. The annual gross value of this additional grain is US$5000 million, based on a world price of $200 per ton. The additional grain is sufficient to supply 180 million people with 1500 calories per day (375 g/day).

The Indian revolution required 5 years of local research, crop testing, and training of farmers to set the stage for the dramatic harvests of 1966–1968, now referred to as the "green revolution." Reports that suggest that the arrival of a shipload of wheat seed is all that is needed for farmers to begin harvesting record crops are mistaken, as India demonstrated.

India can expect to raise its wheat harvest by 50 percent — to 50 million tons or more — during the 1980s and 1990s. Yields from the 11 million hectares of irrigated wheat, which now average 2250 kg/ha, can be raised to 3500 kg/ha, and yields from the 11 million hectares of dryland wheat, which average 750 kg/ha, can be raised to 1100 kg/ha. Both projections are reasonable in the light of experiences elsewhere. These calculations, however, do not take into account a large expansion in irrigated land, which the government of India plans during the 1980s.

A revolution in rice production, closely paralleling that of wheat, occurred in the 1970s, approximately a decade after the wheat revolution. Better farming of wheat and rice then had its impact on the production of still other crops. Double cropping increased rapidly during the 1970s and is still expanding.

Pakistan, in the judgment of CIMMYT's wheat staff, has the

land resources and climate to double its annual wheat production to 20 million tons by the end of the century. This achievement would require continued expansion of irrigation facilities and fertilizer supply and a vigorous research service producing a flow of new, disease-resistant wheat varieties. The government would also need to maintain incentive crop prices for farmers.

The changes that have taken place are a credit to the scientists, policymakers, and political leaders in India and Pakistan who steered the wheat revolution in those countries.

Turkey:
A Dryland Success

Wheat is more important to the economy of Turkey than to the economy of any other developing country. The 45 million Turks annually consume about 200 kilograms of wheat per person, which is among the highest rates in the world. Wheat provides well over half the calories and protein in the diet.

Historically, Turkey has been self-sufficient in cereals and sometimes a major exporter. Mechanization after World War II permitted wheat production to expand enormously. But by 1955 population growth had outpaced the gains in agriculture, and for most of the next 20 years, Turkey had to import wheat.

New varieties and better farming methods began to have an impact on wheat yields in the 1960s. A decade later, as a result of a strong research program and rapid adoption of new technology — and favorable weather — Turkey had five consecutive record wheat harvests. The bumper crops allowed wheat in storage to reach 5 million tons, and exports surged as high as 2 million tons annually.

Turkey's wheat environments

Turkey classifies its wheat-growing areas into nine zones (see Figure 7), but, broadly speaking, there are three major wheat environments: the areas producing winter-habit wheats, the areas producing spring-habit wheats, and the areas producing facultative wheats.

Winter wheats

Winter-habit wheats cover over three quarters of Turkey's wheat land, primarily on the Anatolian plateau, its eastern and southeastern extensions, its transitional zone, and the province of

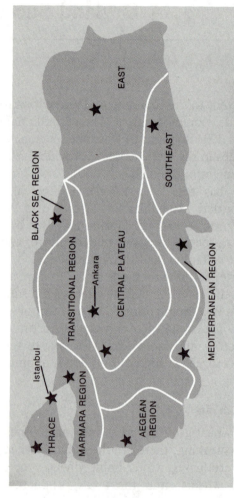

Figure 7. Turkey's wheat-growing areas. Winter wheats cover over 75 percent of the country's 9 million hectares of the crop, primarily on the central plateau, on its eastern and southeastern extensions, and in Thrace. Spring wheats predominate in coastal areas of the Mediterranean, Aegean, Marmara, and Black Sea regions. Facultative wheats are found mainly in the transitional region. Stars indicate locations of wheat research stations.

Thrace. The plateau is a vast, rolling, semi-arid area with a mean elevation of 1000 meters. It normally receives 200 to 450 millimeters of precipitation annually, from October to June. Short localized droughts occur every year, and a prolonged drought strikes about every 8 years. Irrigation is rare on the plateau, and the potential for developing irrigation is slight.

Winter temperatures can be severe, requiring the use of winter-habit wheats. In areas with less than 400 millimeters of precipitation, farmers alternate 1 year of wheat with 1 year of fallow, so only about half the plateau's 12 million hectares of wheat land are planted in any year. The rest is left fallow to accumulate moisture for the following crop. Sheep graze the stubble and weeds during the fallow period. Wheat yields on the plateau have traditionally been low and extremely variable (800 to 1200 kg/ha), but startling gains in recent years have pushed yields up by more than half.

Spring wheats

The second wheat environment is the area of spring-habit wheats, which are primarily planted in autumn in the coastal regions. These regions contain about 1.5 million hectares of wheat. In addition there are scattered patches of spring wheats, grown during the summer, elsewhere in the country, for a total of about 2 million hectares.

In winter the coastal environment offers mild temperatures and 500 to 800 millimeters of rainfall. Here the traditional tall spring wheats gave average yields of 1200 kg/ha before the arrival of Mexican semi-dwarfs in the mid-1960s.

Facultative wheats

Turkey's third wheat environment occurs in the transitional zone and the southeast. These zones plant some "facultative" wheats—types that have a reasonably good cold tolerance but do not require a cold period to induce flowering. The transitional zone has perhaps 600,000 hectares of facultative and winter wheats and 600,000 hectares of spring-habit wheat.

A revolution in three stages

The Turkish wheat revolution has had three stages. The story starts at the end of the World War II, at which time farming in

Turkey had changed little from the days of the Hittites. Oxen or horses were used to draw wooden plows, seed was broadcast by hand, and applying fertilizer on cereal crops was a virtually unknown practice.

Mechanization

Turkey possessed only 1400 tractors in 1946, but under the Marshall Plan 40,000 tractors were imported during the next decade, accompanied by steel plows, disk harrows, grain drills, and grain combines. The new tractor power enabled farmers to cultivate vast areas that had previously been grazing land. Wheat land expanded from about 8 million hectares in 1948 to about 13 million hectares by the mid-1950s (of which nearly half was in fallow each year). Three quarters of the expansion was on the Anatolian plateau — the winter-wheat region. During that period, Turkey's annual wheat production rose about 50 percent to 7 million tons, though yield levels changed little.

Introduction of modern spring wheats

The next stage began when short spring wheats arrived. Two Turkish wheat scientists, who received training in Mexico in 1961 and 1963, carried home the first samples of semi-dwarf wheats. In 1965 a Turkish farmer planted 40 kilograms of seed of the short varieties Sonora 64 and Lerma Rojo 64, which he had obtained from India. The yields so impressed neighboring farmers that a hundred of them banded together and got government approval to order 60 tons of seed from Mexico. This shipment was grown in the 1966–1967 season, and some farmers' yields exceeded 4000 kg/ha, an unheard-of performance in Turkey.

At about the same time, a group of U.S. agricultural consultants visited Turkey at government invitation. They recommended a large purchase of Mexican seed, and the government then imported 22,000 tons of Mexican seed of 12 varieties. The Turkish government also mounted an extension campaign to help farmers apply an effective production package, which included fertilizers, herbicides, and seed treatment. A special feature of the campaign was that the government brought in 12 U.S. wheat farmers and extension agents to work with the Turkish extension service or directly with Turkish farmers.

Within 3 years, the short wheats covered 1.1 million hectares, well over half of Turkey's spring-wheat area. Average yields in the spring-wheat areas continued to increase during the 1970s, reaching 2300 kg/ha in 1976, approximately double the yields of the pre-dwarf period.

New farming practices on the plateau

The environment of the Anatolian plateau required a different strategy for a wheat revolution. Although a change of varieties was the critical need in the lowlands, a change of agronomic practices, primarily for moisture storage and weed control, was essential on the plateau.

In the mid-1960s, the government intensified its research on production methods for the plateau — methods to store more moisture during the fallow period, reduce weeds, and raise soil fertility. Solutions to dryland problems, however, are slower and more difficult to find than those for higher-rainfall areas. In fact 8 years passed before any dramatic change reached the plateau. During this period, the Ministry of Agriculture assigned its top agronomists to work on the wheat problems of the plateau, it sent many scientists abroad for advanced training, and it obtained assistance from an outstanding group of international specialists in developing fallow procedures for the Anatolian plateau.

After hundreds of research trials and demonstrations on farmers' fields, a set of three crop-management procedures emerged. First, during the fallow year, tractor-drawn tillage implements are used to create an insulating stubble mulch on the soil surface, which reduces evaporation but permits moisture to penetrate the soil easily and not run off. Tilling the upper surface of the soil during fallow helps suppress weeds, which would otherwise deplete moisture and nutrients. The fallow period also improves soil fertility as crop residues decay and liberate nutrients.

Second, planting practices were altered considerably. The median planting time in the 2-year cycle was advanced from November to October. Seeds are treated for protection against soil-borne diseases and planted by tractor drill, accompanied by the application of half the required nitrogen fertilizer and all the required phosphorus. This practice gives winter-wheat seedlings a quick start. Their roots develop well, making them strong enough to face cold weather. When these new practices were introduced, some high-yielding winter-wheat varieties were available, notably Bezostaya from the USSR and Bolal, a selection from a U.S. line,

Tractor-drawn tillage equipment has played an important role in the wheat revolution on Turkey's Anatolian plateau. Tillage creates a stubble mulch during the fallow year, reducing moisture losses, suppressing weeds, and increasing soil fertility as crop residues decay. (*Source:* Bill Wright.)

but improved varieties spread more slowly in the highlands than semi-dwarf spring wheats did in the lowlands.

Third, when plant growth resumes in the spring, weeds are knocked out by an application of herbicide, and the crop receives the second half of the nitrogen dose. The three steps are mutually supportive. Moisture stored in the soil is complemented by fertilizer to accelerate seedling growth. Herbicides are used to kill weeds, ensuring that both moisture and nutrients are available to the wheat plants.

The Ministry of Agriculture and the State Planning Organization strongly backed these three steps. The government assigned extension agents to lay out the agronomic trials and thus gave the agents experience for the educational campaign that would follow. Preliminary trials for the new practices were held on research stations, and adaptive research and simple demonstrations followed on farmers' fields. The results from the trials were impressive: The new tillage methods, combined with a modest fertilizer application, added 50 percent to yields.

Table 5
Impact of weather upon wheat yields on the Anatolian plateau of Turkey

		Yield (kg/ha)	
Weather	Chance of occurrence	Traditional technology	Improved technology
Very good	1 year in 8	1,250	3,000
Moderately good	2 years in 8	1,100	2,400
Average	2 years in 8	1,000	2,000
Moderately bad	2 years in 8	900	1,500
Very bad	1 year in 8	750	1,250
Avg., all years		1,000	2,000

Source: Adapted from Charles K. Mann, 1977, The impact of technology on wheat production in Turkey.

Research showed that merely adding herbicide to traditional production practices could raise harvests by nearly 20 percent, and if the herbicide treatment was precisely timed, the increase in yield was as much as 48 percent. Cost/benefit research showed that applying herbicide was highly profitable. For each lira the farmer spent on herbicide, he received increased returns of 4.4 lira.

During 1975–1977 the government extension staff intensified its campaign to persuade highland farmers to adopt the new production package, and this period was the start of five consecutive record harvests. An important aspect of the improved technology in the risky plateau environment is that it works in bad years as well as good ones. Using weather records for 1946–1975, an economist developed five weather classifications, which he related to yield data from on-farm testing of the old and the new technologies. The study showed that improved technology gives higher yields in all types of years (see Table 5), but in years of better weather, the payoff from improved technology widens substantially. In the long run, average yields under improved technology are twice as large as average yields under traditional technology.

Overview of the revolution

Turkey's postwar gains in wheat production have been remarkable. At a world price of US$200/ton, the wheat crop was worth over US$2700 million more in 1979 than it was in 1950. Higher input use, much of it for wheat, contributed greatly to that

Table 6
Turkey: Wheat production and input use for all crops, 1946–1979

	Wheat					
Year	Yield (kg/ha)	Area (000 ha)	Production (000 tons)	Fertilizer[a] (000 tons)	Herbicides[b] (tons)	Tractors (000's)
1946	952	3,831	3,648	nil	nil	1
1950	864	4,477	3,872	8	nil	17
1955	977	7,060	6,900	28	7	40
1960	1,097	7,700	8,450	21	114	42
1965	1,075	7,900	8,500	163	411	55
1970	1,163	8,600	10,000	443	1,307	106
1975	1,595	9,245	14,750	738	1,704	263
1979	1,896	9,300	17,631	932[c]	3,201[c]	312[c]

[a]Nutrient weight. [b]Active ingredient. [c]1976 (latest data available).

Sources: Adapted from Charles K. Mann, 1977, The impact of technology on wheat production in Turkey. Data for 1979 from FAO *Production yearbook.*

success (see Table 6). Consumption of fertilizer rose from near zero to more than 900,000 tons by the end of the 1970s. The use of herbicides rose from nothing to 3200 tons, which is enough to control weeds on 3.2 million hectares. Tractors increased to 312,000 units, and some of the mechanization in the 1960s and 1970s was paid for by the profits from wheat.

Another important factor was the excellent corps of wheat scientists Turkey developed. That group remained essentially intact during the 1970s, a period in which the government changed 12 times. Continuity of scientists reinforced results, and when the foreign specialists went home, they left in place a skilled and experienced wheat staff.

Employment was stimulated by the wheat revolution. Hundreds of small ironworking shops sprang up to provide the plows, harrows, sweeps, and sprayers required by wheat farmers, and this small industry employed many new workers. Wheat farms, too, required more labor to apply the increased amount of inputs used and to bring in the larger harvests.

Some issues in the wheat revolution

The changes in Turkish wheat production had a far-reaching impact. The effect on sheep production and the problems in managing a wheat stockpile were two issues agricultural policymakers had to deal with.

Sheep versus wheat

Most of Turkey's 40 million sheep graze stubble and weeds on fallow land in the 2-year wheat-fallow rotation. Farmers were fearful that the recommended tillage practices to conserve moisture and control weeds would reduce the amount of forage for sheep and, thus, the income from sheep. The revolution in wheat production has upset the equilibrium in the old wheat-sheep balance, and in time, the revolution may stimulate new technology for sheep production. There is new interest in forage research.

Wheat stockpile

Turkey's wheat stocks began rising in 1975 and had reached 5 million tons by 1980. During that period, wheat exports ranged from 0.8 million to 2 million tons a year. The government stockpile serves as a food reserve, and part has been deliberately withheld from the world market while awaiting higher prices. This grain reserve contains many hidden costs. The fertilizer and herbicides used on wheat are subsidized, the government credit programs under which the crop is grown involve some loss, and the government absorbs the low storage costs.

But there are offsetting factors. The government's investment is in Turkish lira, and the foreign sales are in hard currency. Since much of the land where winter wheat is grown will not support other cultivated crops, and since there is an extreme shortage of foreign exchange, producing wheat for export makes sense. If both inputs and outputs are valued at international prices, Turkey is a competitive producer of wheat.

Looking ahead

Turkey inevitably will have some bad wheat years because of droughts, but there seems little doubt that yields of wheats on the Anatolian plateau will continue to increase, probably to 2000 kg/ha or more, because only about half the farmers of the plateau had adopted the recommended practices by 1980. Also, more benefit can be expected from higher-yielding winter wheats. The government released three varieties of winter wheats in 1979 — two bread wheats and one durum. The yield potential of these new varieties is 4000 to 5000 kg/ha compared with 2000 to 2500 kg/ha for many earlier varieties.

Spring-wheat yields are likely to rise from 2300 kg/ha to 3000 kg/ha or more by 1990, since semi-dwarf wheats were grown only on about 75 percent of the lowland wheat area in 1980 and new higher-yielding varieties can be expected in future years. These projections suggest that wheat production in Turkey could surpass 25 million tons by 1990.

To stabilize wheat production at a high level, while keeping stockpile costs reasonable, Turkey could take several actions. First, it could reduce agricultural subsidies (a political step that the government is reluctant to take). Second, it could promote alternative uses for some wheat land. Coastal areas could shift from wheat to winter oilseeds or berseem clover. The steeper plateau lands could be removed from cultivation and seeded to improved pasture species for grazing. Some of these changes are already occurring, but the pace could be speeded by research and by price incentives. Third, the government could step up its wheat exports. Turkey has some advantage in transport costs for sales to Mideast countries and the USSR. It may also be able to expand its share in the durum markets of Italy and North Africa.

Bangladesh, China, Brazil, and Argentina

The four national wheat programs discussed in this chapter each illustrate special accomplishments:

- Bangladesh developed wheat as an important supplement to its diet, which consists predominantly of rice.
- China raised its average annual wheat output to 58 million tons during 1978–1980, making it the world's second-largest wheat producer (after the USSR).
- Brazil nearly doubled its wheat production in the 1970s — mainly by clearing and cultivating previously unused land — despite acid soils, numerous wheat diseases, erratic rainfall, and unseasonable frosts.
- Argentina is the most successful wheat exporter in the Third World, having sold abroad an average of 3.7 million tons of wheat annually during 1975–1979.

BANGLADESH: A NEWCOMER TO WHEAT

Bangladesh, a nation of rice eaters, is adding wheat to its diet, and its scientists and farmers are making surprising progress with the crop. During the 1970s, the area under wheat tripled, the average wheat yield more than doubled, and the wheat harvest increased 800 percent (see Table 7). Most of the added wheat area came from planting rice land that had been left idle in the dry season. Large areas have insufficient water for a dry-season rice crop, yet residual soil moisture or irrigation from low-lift pumps can support wheat. (A rice crop would require 800 to 1600 millimeters of water, but a wheat crop needs only 300 to 450 millimeters.)

Table 7
Bangladesh: Wheat expansion and imports, 1961–1980

Period	Area (000 ha)	Yield (kg/ha)	Production (000 tons)	Imports (000 tons)
1961–1965 avg	61	623	38	458
1966–1970 avg	87	690	60	761
1971–1975 avg	121	826	100	1,621
1976	150	1,453	218	1,173
1977	158	1,639	259	623
1978	202	1,698	343	1,331
1979	265	1,864	494	1,123
1980	430	1,884	810	1,189

Sources: 1961–1979 from FAO *Production yearbook* and FAO *Trade yearbook;* 1980 from Bangladesh Agricultural Research Institute.

Urgent factors have propelled the wheat expansion. First, in the 1970s, the population of Bangladesh rose from 75 to 91 million, and production of the principal food crop, rice, did not keep pace. Second, Bangladesh suffers from a severe land-pressure problem: There are 10 persons for each hectare of cropland (only Egypt with 15 persons per hectare and South Korea with 18 persons per hectare have a higher density among the developing countries). Third, the food deficit in Bangladesh persists despite production campaigns. Wheat has been imported every year from 1960 to 1980, and recent increases in wheat production have only begun to moderate grain imports.

Modern varieties

Bangladesh was a slow starter with modern wheats. In 1970 when the semi-dwarfs covered millions of hectares in India and West Pakistan, they evoked little interest in East Pakistan (which became Bangladesh in 1971), probably because wheat was a minor crop and because government officials generally felt that the public's preference for rice was unshakable.

But several events raised the government's interest in wheat. The taste for bread had been growing. During the 1960s, large amounts of wheat were imported on concessional terms to meet food-grain deficits. Moreover, short-statured wheats began to be introduced into East Pakistan by breeders from West Pakistan in 1965. Testing began on experiment stations, but little seed reached the farmers.

Starting in 1969, a few wheat scientists were trained in Mexico. When these trainees returned, they demonstrated that semi-dwarf wheat varieties could yield 2000 to 3000 kg/ha in the dry winter season, even without irrigation, and 4000 to 5000 kg/ha with irrigation. Nevertheless in 1973, when a team from CIMMYT visited Bangladesh and urged a national wheat campaign, the idea received a cold response. A severe shortage of rice in 1973, however, proved to be a turning point. Bangladesh was forced to import 2.5 million tons of wheat at a cost of US$340 million. When a CIMMYT team visited the next year, all doors were open. The Ministry of Agriculture decided to import 4000 tons of seed of the modern varieties to launch a wheat campaign in 1975, which led, step by step, to a harvest of 800,000 tons in 1980.

Factors of success

Officials in Bangladesh cite a dozen factors as contributing to the effectiveness of the wheat campaign. If any factor had been neglected, results would have been reduced.

Staff development

In the late 1970s, Bangladesh sent five wheat scientists per year to Mexico for training. Upon returning home, these young scientists manned the research stations and seed farms and conducted training courses.

Testing new varieties

Bangladesh decided not to breed its own wheat varieties at the outset. Instead, it tested wheats imported from India, Pakistan, Mexico, and elsewhere. By this process, researchers identified ten varieties for release, including such well-known names as Sonora 64, INIA 66, Tanori 71, Jupateco 73, and Pavon 76 from Mexico and Kalyansona and Sonalika from India. In 1979 Bangladesh released two varieties, Balaka and Doel, that had resulted from reselections made in Bangladesh from one Indian and one Mexican line.

Agronomic research

Older scientists, reinforced by trainees returning from Mexico, conducted the needed agronomic trials on farms: date and rate of seeding, fertilizer application, and so forth. Agronomic work was shortened by first utilizing data from similar trials in the neighboring Indian state of West Bengal.

Seed supply

Bangladesh imported 7500 tons of wheat seed between 1975 and 1979, mainly Sonalika from India. In 1980, 33,000 tons of seed were imported from Mexico, the United States, and India to expand the area planted to wheat.

The quality of seed multiplied on government farms was poor when the wheat campaign was launched. The Agricultural Development Corporation took steps to improve the situation by sending managers of seed farms to Mexico for training. When they returned, they changed cultural practices and altered storage methods to safeguard seed against monsoon humidity. The seed program now receives assistance from the FAO, the Federal Republic of Germany, and the World Bank. Bangladesh will continue to import wheat seed while it is expanding its wheat crop to cover an additional half million hectares, but once the crop area is stabilized, the country will be self-sufficient in seed.

Demonstration plots

Both research and extension staffs participated in laying out hundreds of demonstration plots on private farms. This activity was well publicized on radio and in the press.

Fertilizer

Use of fertilizer for all crops in Bangladesh reached 400,000 tons (of nutrients) in 1980, double the amount used 5 years earlier. The country uses local natural gas to produce most of its nitrogen fertilizer, but it will need to expand its production greatly to keep pace with the wheat campaign. All phosphorus fertilizer is imported.

Irrigation

Bangladesh exploits many forms of irrigation, including storage dams, stream diversion, low-lift pumps on canals, and tubewells (mostly shallow wells that are privately owned and operated with diesel-powered or hand pumps). Irrigated land expanded from

700,000 hectares in 1975 to 1.2 million hectares in 1980, but that is still only 13 percent of the total cropland. Irrigation will become increasingly important as wheat spreads beyond the areas that have a high water table or abundant residual moisture.

Price supports

Before each planting season, Bangladesh sets a guaranteed price for wheat that is close to the world price. The price is high enough to encourage expansion of the wheat area and the use of substantial amounts of fertilizer.

Storage

Most wheat produced in Bangladesh is consumed by the farmers who grow it or is moved only short distances to local markets. The government has demonstrated how farmers can construct inexpensive home storage bins for wheat. More storage in market towns will be needed as local wheat replaces more of the imports.

Planning techniques

The campaign in Bangladesh uses comprehensive planning techniques. Targets are set for each wheat-growing district. Plans specify the number of hectares of wheat to be grown, the varieties to be grown, the local requirements for seed and fertilizer, the dates of delivery for inputs, the number of local demonstrations, the schedule for staff training, and the name of the officer responsible for each target. The system sounds bureaucratic, but it works.

Foreign aid

Bangladesh has made use of foreign aid for training its wheat staff, for importing seed, for building fertilizer factories, for purchasing irrigation equipment, and for planning.

Support from political leadership

Political leaders have supported the wheat campaign with speeches, press interviews, awards to government scientists, and ceremonies recognizing farmers who win local yield contests. Political backing will be vital as the country carries out its plans to double the area and production of wheat by 1985.

CHINA: LARGEST WHEAT GROWER IN THE THIRD WORLD

China's wheat statistics dwarf those of most countries. Between 1950 and 1980, according to government announcements, China's wheat area expanded from 23 million to 29 million hectares, its average wheat yield rose from 600 kg/ha to as high as 2130 kg/ha, and its wheat production climbed from 15 million tons to a peak of 62.7 million tons in 1979. The bases for these gains are not fully apparent because visitors have been shown the more prosperous Yangtze Valley, Yellow River Valley, and coastal plains, but they have not seen many of the less advanced areas.

Distribution and types of wheat

China produces wheat from a latitude of 53 degrees north on the Siberian border to the tropics (18 degrees north on Hainan Island). Consequently China requires varieties for a broad range of temperature regimes and in a wide range of maturity classes.

China's wheat crop is almost entirely bread wheats. About 60 percent of China's commercial wheat crop is winter-habit wheat, and the rest is spring wheat (perhaps half the spring crop is actually facultative wheat, which is not separately measured). Large areas of spring wheat are grown in all major wheat regions (see Figure 8) except the northern plains; it is planted in the autumn except in the northeast. Winter wheat is important in the northwest and northern plains. Significant amounts of facultative wheat are found in the northern plains, the southwest, and the Yangtze region.

Wheat diseases

Wheat breeders in China say they have not had a stem or leaf rust epidemic since the 1950s. Stripe rust, however, caused an epidemic in northern China in 1964 and remains a constant threat in the winter-wheat areas and in the southwest. Wheat varieties are replaced frequently in those regions as a safeguard against stripe rust.

The most damaging disease in the spring-wheat areas is scab (fusarium) in the Yangtze Valley. Scab causes losses every year, estimated at 10 percent in the spring-wheat areas, and a severe epidemic occurs every 4 to 5 years. A few breeding materials with

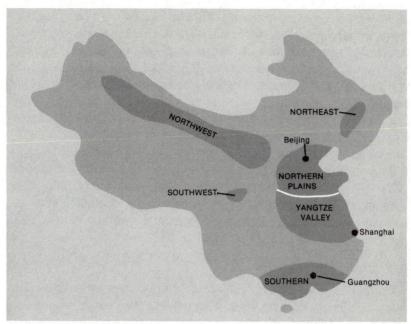

Figure 8. China's wheat-growing areas. Every Chinese province grows wheat, but of the 29 million hectares of wheat, over 12 million are in the North China plains, approximately 6 million are in the northwest, and another 5 million are in the central and lower Yangtze Valley. Lesser concentrations are located in the northeast and in the southwest, mainly in the Sichuan basin. Fewer than 1 million hectares are in the southern region.

mild resistance to scab have been identified in China, but the genes for resistance have not yet been pyramided and transferred to more desirable plant types.

Factors in China's wheat expansion

The major factors of growth in the Chinese wheat crop are not difficult to identify for the great river valleys and the coastal plains where most progress is said to have occurred.

Cropland improvement

For three decades, China conducted a vast rural reconstruction program in the winter, formerly the idle season, by forming the rural population into a labor force. Cropland was leveled, small dams were built, irrigation and drainage canals were dug, hillsides were terraced or reforested, and farm-to-market roads were constructed. These activities transformed 35 million hectares, a third of China's cropland, into areas of "high and stable yields"—to use the government's phrase. These areas suffer less risk of drought because of irrigation or because rainfall is reliable; the risk of flooding is diminished through drainage and water control. China's 29 million hectares of wheat land lie mainly in the areas of "high and stable yield."

The stability of wheat production met a severe test during 1979–1980 when the North China plains experienced the driest autumn and winter in 40 years. Despite the drought, national wheat production dipped only 16 percent below the record 1979 crop.

Improved wheat varieties

China has more than a dozen research institutes at work on new wheat varieties. Most winter-wheat areas are sown with high-yielding semi-dwarf varieties developed in China. Chinese scientists have gathered the best winter-wheat varieties from North America and Europe for making crosses. One series of winter varieties—Taishan 1, 4, and 5—has yielded 7000 to 9000 kg/ha under experimental conditions. These varieties cover over 3 million hectares in the North China plains.

China imported 19,700 tons of seed of Mexican spring wheats in 1973–1974, and the short plant type now predominates in China's spring-wheat areas. Mexican wheats have been extensively used as parents in crosses with Chinese spring wheats, to combine the best features of both.

Fertilizers

Historically China has used more organic fertilizer than any other country (composts made from crop residue, animal manure, night soil, and river silt). Organic fertilizer is now supplemented by chemical fertilizers. Ammonium bicarbonate is produced from coal in hundreds of small factories. Single superphosphate is made from local phosphate rock, and sulfuric acid is derived from local pyrites. High-formula nitrogen fertilizers are becoming available. China has constructed 13 giant factories, each capable of producing 1000 tons of ammonia a day, and most of them were operating by 1980. China appears to have tripled its consumption of

Farmers in North China spreading unthreshed wheat on a highway to speed drying. (*Source:* CIMMYT.)

chemical fertilizer during the 1970s to about 100 kilograms of nutrients per hectare of cropland.

Extension

Research institutes in China have decentralized their verification trials to the countryside (that is, to the commune level), and thus they have speeded the adoption of recommended wheat varieties and production methods. China now has one of the most effective extension services in the world because it can move new ideas more rapidly and achieve adoption by farmers more completely.

Multiple cropping

China has intensified its cropping patterns. Twelve-month sequences such as rice-rice-barley or rice-rice-wheat are used in southern China and the Yangtze Valley; maize-wheat, in North China; and vegetables-wheat, in Northeast China. These sequences make maximum use of arable land and solar radiation throughout the year. Triple cropping has diminished in some areas because two long-season grain crops grown in 12 months produce almost the same output as three short-maturity crops, and with less labor.

Double cropping continues to be practiced wherever moisture permits. These efficient cropping patterns have been aided by China's exceptional success in breeding early-maturing varieties. In winter wheats, good winterhardiness has been combined with earliness.

China has also promoted relay cropping—planting seeds or seedlings between the rows of a ripening crop so that the second crop is well started before the first is harvested. China's "cropping index" is now estimated at 1.50; that is, each hectare of cropland produces an average of 1.5 crops a year.

Agronomic practices

Agronomists in China have designed significant improvements in wheat production practices. Winter-wheat planting dates have been made earlier because new shorter-season summer crops can be harvested earlier in the autumn. Wheat seeding rates have been raised in some areas from 75 to 150 kg/ha (though some outsiders consider this rate too high). Irrigation schedules have been adjusted to closely match the times when the wheat plants need maximum moisture.

A large remaining agronomic problem is the production and incorporation of organic material. Heavy application of compost on spring wheat at planting (when soil temperatures are low) appears to starve the crop of nutrients in the first 30 days of growth—the slow oxidation of organic matter at this time temporarily ties up soil nutrients—and thus this practice reduces tillering in the wheat plant and lowers the number of spikelets. This problem is severe in the colder areas of the northeast.

And the future?

There is a good prospect that China can raise its wheat yields 50 percent before the end of the century—to 3200 kg/ha or more. These further gains could bring a harvest of 90 million to 100 million tons of wheat. Higher yields would be made possible by using varieties with better disease resistance (especially to scab), applying more chemical fertilizer, and extending irrigation.

If scab-tolerant wheat varieties can be developed (see Chapter 9), not only will China's wheat harvest increase substantially, grain quality will also improve. Periodic scab epidemics now make part of the wheat grown in the Yangtze Valley unusable for either food or feed.

BRAZIL: A PROGRAM WITH EXTREME SOIL
AND DISEASE PROBLEMS

Brazil's imports of wheat averaged 3 million tons annually during the 1970s. This is the largest wheat deficit in Latin America, and wheat consumption in Brazil continues to increase dramatically. Yet Brazil's potential for expanding its wheat area may be greater than that of any other country.

Brazil's energetic farmers opened new land at a rapid rate during the 1970s, primarily to produce soybeans. The soybean growers often plant wheat as a winter cover crop to prevent erosion and to provide some income. As a result of the expansion of soybean production, over half of the 3.2 million hectares on which Brazil grows wheat (see Figure 9) has been opened since 1970.

Wheat yields, however, average only 800 kg/ha, and they fluctuate from year to year between 500 and 1000 kg/ha. Four severe problems cause the low and unstable yields. First, much of the wheat is grown in acid soil, and the high levels of soluble aluminum and strong phosphorus fixation in these soils depress yields. Second, in Brazil wheat is attacked by nearly every wheat disease except stripe rust (one survey counted 37 diseases). Classic epidemics of stem and leaf rust, septoria, fusarium head blight, mildew, and helminthosporium occurred during the 1970s. Third, rainfall is sometimes too little, but more often too much, particularly near harvest, thus encouraging fungus diseases. Fourth, unseasonable frosts strike periodically. Frosts were destructive 2 years out of 10 in the 1970s. An aggressive research program is beginning to mitigate some of these problems.

Acid soils

Large areas of Brazil's soils are strongly acid. These soils contain free aluminum, which inhibits the growth of the roots of most wheat varieties, resulting in reduced tillering and low yields. In acid soils, too, phosphorus, an essential nutrient, is not freely available to the plant roots. Fortunately Brazil has long had a few wheat varieties that tolerate acid soils and are able to extract soil phosphorus under acid conditions. But the yield of these hardy plants is low, generally 600 to 800 kg/ha.

In 1973 Brazilian scientists and CIMMYT organized a joint research program that aimed at combining the aluminum tolerance

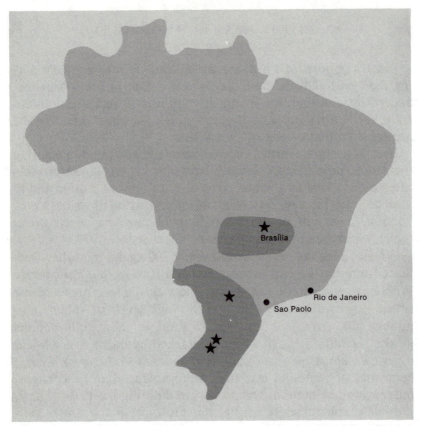

Figure 9. Brazil's wheat-growing areas. Over 90 percent of Brazil's 3.2 million hectares of wheat are in the south. About 3 percent is around Brasília. Major wheat-research centers are indicated by a star.

of Brazil's wheats with the stem and leaf rust resistance and high-yield potential of Mexican wheats. Since the parental materials for Mexican short wheats are in Mexico, crosses with Brazilian wheats are made in Mexico. Seeds from the crosses are flown to Brazil to be planted in trials in the acid soils. Seeds selected from plants that show desirable characteristics are then flown back to Mexico to be used in subsequent cycles of crossing and selection. Because the seeds fly back and forth twice a year, the procedure has been called "shuttle breeding."

The Brazilian-Mexican breeding program uncovered an interesting plant characteristic. Because Alondra, a Mexican variety, grows well in Brazil, it was first presumed to be highly tolerant to acid soils and to aluminum toxicity. But subsequent testing showed that Alondra is only moderately tolerant to aluminum toxicity. Its outstanding performance in Brazil, it was found, stems from an ability to extract phosphorus from acid soils. This characteristic is genetically controlled, and many progeny from crosses with Alondra now have it.

Septoria and scab

Along with raising the aluminum tolerance of Brazilian wheats, a second step will be to incorporate better resistance to two fungus diseases, septoria (leaf and head blotch) and scab (fusarium). These are the most destructive diseases of wheat in Brazil.

Septoria is common in Mediterranean climates. Two pathogens, *Septoria tritici* and *Septoria nodorum*, have been identified, and both are prevalent in Brazil. *S. nodorum* uses the subtropical grasses in Brazil as an alternate host. Moreover, the pathogen is apparently changing constantly through sexual crosses and mutation, so development of resistance to septoria is not easy. Considerable progress has nevertheless been made, particularly against *S. tritici*. CIMMYT, in collaboration with Israel, Turkey, Argentina, and several other countries, has been assembling and intercrossing genes for resistance.

For scab, the most promising sources of tolerance are certain Argentine, Japanese, and Chinese varieties, which generally have a poor plant type. CIMMYT has been attempting to bring these genetic sources together in the hope of increasing their resistance level (see Chapter 9).

By 1981 a few high-yielding lines in the Brazil-CIMMYT program appeared to combine aluminum tolerance with resistance to the three rusts, plus septoria, scab, and helminthosporium. If this combination of resistance holds up in worldwide testing, the Brazilian work could prove a breakthrough for wheat in the tropics.

A cost/benefit question

The improvement of wheats for Brazilian conditions is a demanding undertaking, but the potential gains justify it. Brazil has 250 million hectares of acid soils, the *campo cerrado* (a tree-bush-grass ecosystem). This is the largest underutilized block of agricultural land in the world. Much of this area might be suited for a soybean-wheat rotation or other summer-winter crop combinations if wheat varieties can be developed that are tolerant to acid soils and capable of extracting phosphorus from them. Supplemental irrigation would also be needed.

Similar blocks of acid soils exist in Africa (Zaire, Zimbabwe, Kenya, Tanzania, Zambia, and Mozambique) and in Southeast Asia (Burma, Thailand, Malaysia, and Indonesia). Possibly the results of the work in Brazil can be transferred to other countries. At the least, the results will greatly reduce the amount of research necessary in Africa and Asia.

ARGENTINA: A MAJOR EXPORTER

Argentina is the largest wheat exporter in the Third World. From 1960 to 1980, Argentina exported at least a million tons of wheat every year. Recently Argentina's exports have reached almost 4 million tons a year out of a total wheat harvest of 8 million tons. Yields currently average 1600 kg/ha.

The Argentine exports are made possible by an excellent climate and good soils for wheat, outstanding farmers, ample land (about 1 hectare of arable land per capita), a well-qualified research staff at INTA (the National Institute of Agricultural Technology), and efficient private seed companies that add to the steady flow of seeds of high-yielding wheat varieties.

Officials estimate that 80 percent of Argentina's 5 million hectares of wheat are planted to semi-dwarf varieties. Some varieties, like Marco Juarez INTA (a product of Mexican-Argentine cooperative breeding in the 1960s), are widely used in the breeding programs of other countries, particularly for disease resistance. Moreover, the early maturity of the short wheats has made it possible for some Argentine farmers to adopt a soybean-wheat rotation, which now covers more than 1 million hectares.

Argentina could produce even larger wheat surpluses in the 1980s if it modified two policies: First, the government maintains a monopoly on the export of wheat and pays the farmer a price that is well below the world price. Second, a tariff on imported nitrogen fertilizer keeps the domestic price higher than the world price, thus discouraging the use of fertilizer. Despite having an abundance of natural gas, Argentina has not developed a nitrogen fertilizer industry.

As the world population grows, Argentina can be expected to provide even larger exports.

Elements of an Effective National Wheat Program

The national wheat efforts described in the preceding chapters demonstrate that wheat improvement can be achieved under widely differing environmental, economic, social, and political conditions. Although no two programs are alike, there are some common elements for success (see Table 8). Most wheat-growing countries already employ some of them, but any developing country whose dryland wheat averages less than 1000 kg/ha or whose irrigated wheat averages less than 2000 kg/ha has not yet succeeded in putting the elements together. Something is missing or something is being done ineffectively.

Joining a wheat network

Virtually all countries with successful wheat programs participate in one or more wheat research and testing networks. A network consists of the participants in international nurseries who test the same varieties and experimental lines, exchange research data, and take part in international workshops. A nursery is a collection of wheat varieties and advanced lines that is grown at many locations to compare characteristics such as yield, earliness, and disease resistance. Reliable comparisons between entries in a nursery can be made only if the seed used at each location comes from the same source and uniform production practices are followed at each location. Five organizations that distribute international nurseries are listed in the Appendix.

Typical activities of a network are the following:

- A country requests the seeds for international nurseries, grows them, submits its results, and receives annual nursery

Table 8
Checklist of elements in an effective wheat-production program

Identifying the wheat-growing zones

Problem-oriented research with a team approach
    Training a critical mass of researchers
    Development of modern wheat varieties
    Off-season breeding cycle
    Agronomic research
    On-farm trials
    Early warning for new disease pathogens
    Cereal technology laboratory

Plant quarantine service

Availability of inputs
    Seed services
    Fertilizers
    Irrigation, drainage, electricity for pumping
    Herbicides, insecticides, fungicides
    Farm implements and traction

Agricultural extension
    Training the extension agent
    Transportation for the agent
    On-farm demonstrations, field days, contests
    Maximizing extension contacts
    Maintaining extension morale

Economic policies for a wheat program
    Farm credit
    Price supports
    Input subsidies
    Wheat imports
    Food subsidies
    Budgeting for the wheat program

Dealing with an oversupply of wheat
    Food reserves and storage
    Exports
    Feed and industrial uses
    Food-for-work programs
    Promoting substitute crops

Farmers' service organizations

Psychological factors

Dynamic program leader

reports, enabling it to identify the wheats best adapted to its environment. Nurseries are the most important channel for distributing the world's newest and best wheats. Any participant may release nursery materials as varieties or use them for further crossing.

- Wheat scientists from leading research institutions visit countries in the network to discuss wheat problems.
- Workshops are organized among wheat scientists in the network, usually on a regional basis. National wheat-research programs are reviewed at these meetings, and plans for the next year's nurseries are discussed. Participants suggest varieties to be included.
- Fellowships for scientific training are arranged through the network.
- Publications on wheat are made available through the network.

Identifying wheat-growing zones

The administrator of a national wheat program needs to know the country's present and potential wheat-growing regions and their limiting factors. The features that distinguish the regions are important in selecting wheat varieties, in planning fertilizer supplies, and in deciding where to invest in irrigation.

Wheat regions can be mapped from four types of information. First, moisture information will permit classifying wheat areas as well watered, semi-arid, fully irrigated, or partially irrigated. The pattern of rainfall distribution throughout the year is important. Next comes temperature data—mean temperature during the wheat-growing season, maximum and minimum temperatures by months, the date of the last killing frost in the spring and the first killing frost in the autumn (where applicable), and the date for the onset of hot, dry winds.

Then come soil types, such as deep clay or loam soils, which hold moisture well; sandy soils, which quickly lose their moisture; shallow eroded soils; or problem soils, such as saline soils or soils that are high in aluminum. Finally, regions are distinguished by the prevalent diseases, insects, weeds, birds, and rodents, which influence the choice of wheat varieties and the recommendation of production practices.

The wheat administrator, after reviewing information on moisture, temperature, soils, and pests, will ensure that his staff delineates a manageable number of zones. China, for example, has selected eight regions for its 29 million hectares of wheat land; India uses ten regions for 22 million hectares; Turkey uses nine regions; and Mexico, three.

It is a fortunate administrator who has a map of his country's wheat-growing zones, listing their characteristics, the hectares of wheat in each, the average yield, and the problems to be attacked by research and extension. Defining wheat-growing zones is the first step in formulating priorities for wheat research. Research funds are a scarce resource and need to be allocated by a system of priorities.

Problem-oriented research with a team approach

Any country that has 200,000 hectares of rainfed wheat or 100,000 hectares of irrigated wheat can justify supporting one or more research stations for adaptive wheat trials. Such areas should produce a wheat crop of at least 200,000 tons, which would be worth US$40 million or more. If 1 percent of the crop value were assigned to research, there would be a research budget of US$400,000 a year.

Wheat research is normally organized by climatic regions. That is why the mapping of wheat zones is so important. In Mexico, India, and Turkey, research centers have been established in each climatic zone. At first these regional stations operated independently of each other, but to raise their effectiveness, they subsequently were drawn together in problem-oriented research by joint activities such as national nursery trials, national workshops, national farmer contests, and national awards for civil servants.

Problem-oriented research should also address aspects of economic policy (that is, identification of obstacles to growth). The sooner the economic constraints are identified, the better for the program.

Development of modern wheat varieties

Eight out of ten developing countries that produce wheat are growing varieties imported from other countries with satisfactory

At CIMMYT, 38 wheat nurseries are assembled annually for distribution to over a hundred countries. (*Source:* CIMMYT.)

results. They select outstanding varieties from international nurseries, multiply the seed, and give the varieties local names. About one in ten wheat-growing nations use wheat varieties that they have improved themselves by reselecting from exotic advanced-generation populations received from CIMMYT and other wheat research centers. Reselection is most often used to obtain better resistance to local diseases. The rest of the wheat-growing developing countries create varieties by crossing and selection. Often the crosses are between the best imported lines and the leading local varieties. Crossing requires a larger trained staff and a longer period to achieve results.

The foregoing classification of countries can be restated on the basis of national crop area. That is, the developing countries that create varieties through crossing programs (Argentina, China, India, Mexico, Pakistan, and Turkey are examples) have about 80 percent of the wheat area; the countries that practice reselection from exotic populations have about 10 percent of the wheat area; and the countries that test wheat varieties from the world network and release suitable ones without modification have the remaining 10 percent of the area.

This situation is unsurprising. Countries that have a large wheat area tend to have large economies, which can support sizable research budgets, including a wheat-breeding staff. By contrast, countries with small economies can afford only a limited agricultural budget and staff. For them it is wise to make maximum use of the breeding services of the international networks. Even a large country like Brazil, which is well staffed with wheat researchers, finds it advantageous to conduct a joint breeding program with an international center, thus pooling its resources with those of the networks.

For countries that can justify a wheat-breeding program, a crossing block is essential. A crossing block is a collection of wheat varieties and advanced lines selected to serve as parents in a breeding program. Each entry is chosen to contribute one or more characteristics such as high yield, short plant height, early maturity, or resistance to a disease. Entries in the crossing block are grown in the same season on neighboring plots, and planting dates are staggered to bring the entries into flowering at approximately the same time, thus facilitating pollination. Some of the strongest donor parents in CIMMYT's 1981 crossing block for spring wheats are listed in Table 9.

Off-season breeding cycle

Most developing countries that engage in wheat breeding have one breeding cycle per year, but countries that are making rapid breeding progress have two cycles. Countries that have suitable environments for growing two spring-wheat cycles each year include Mexico, the Andean countries of South America, Kenya, Tanzania, Turkey, Iran, Afghanistan, Pakistan, India, Nepal, and China. Breeders in other countries can grow two cycles of spring wheat by sending seeds abroad. For example, countries in the Mediterranean basin and the Mideast can utilize Kenya's Njoro station for a summer cycle, and some countries of Latin America utilize facilities in Mexico. More rapid breeding progress could be achieved if more developing countries doubled their annual research cycles for wheat. This doubling is usually not possible for winter-habit wheats, however.

Table 9
The CIMMYT crossing block, 1981: Outstanding varieties used as sources of selected spring bread-wheat characteristics

Short plant height	Stem rust resistance
Yecora 70 (Mexico)	Gamut (Australia)
Torim 73 (Mexico)	Era (U.S.)
Cajeme 71 (Mexico)	Timagalen (Australia)
	Glenlea (Canada)
High yield	Torim 73 (Mexico)
Nacozari 76 (Mexico)	
Pavon 76 (Mexico)	Leaf rust resistance
Siete Cerros 66 (Mexico)	Tezanos Pintos Precoz (Argentina)
Anza (U.S.)	Era (U.S.)
Yecora 70 (Mexico)	Gaboto (Argentina)
Early maturity	Stripe rust resistance
INIA 66 (Mexico)	Bonza (Colombia)
Sonalika (India)	Andes (Colombia)
	Bananaquit (Mexico)
High protein content	
CIANO 67 (Mexico)	Resistance to *Septoria tritici*
Calidad (Mexico)	Bobwhite "S" (Mexico)
Naphal (Nepal)	CNT 7 (Brazil)
	Colonias (Brazil)
Large amber grains	
Sonalika (India)	Aluminum tolerance
HD832 (India)	Maringa (Brazil)
	Paso Fundo 10100 (Brazil)
Milling and baking quality	Pelota 72380 (Brazil)
Azteca 67 (Mexico)	Arthur 71 (U.S.)
Era (U.S.)	PAT 73121 (Brazil)
INIA 66 (Mexico)	Alondra (Mexico)

Agronomic research

Appropriate production practices vary not only between countries, but also between wheat-growing zones within each country. Therefore every research service should conduct trials on time of sowing, date and rate of seeding, fertilizer rates and placement, timing of irrigations, methods of weed control, crop rotations, and other agronomic practices. These trials are the basis for recommendations to farmers. The resulting package of practices will speed farmers' acceptance of new varieties and new technologies.

On-farm trials

Researchers have to conduct some wheat trials on farmers' fields because farm production conditions are different from those on the experiment station. On-farm trials serve several purposes. First, they test the performance of new varieties and agronomic practices. Second, they permit farmers to observe the performance of new varieties and practices on their land and under their own conditions, thus giving greater credibility to research findings. Third, on-farm trials put the researcher in direct contact with farmers' problems, which influences the course of subsequent research. Fourth, results from on-farm trials can improve the decision makers' understanding of farm conditions and potentials.

Early warning for new disease pathogens

A warning system for monitoring new races of wheat diseases covers about 20 countries between India and Morocco. A similar system exists in South America. The original system was set up in India in the 1960s; then CIMMYT, with support from international donors, expanded it internationally. The warning system operates with "trap nurseries," which are identical sets of popular commercial varieties planted at many sites in a region. Scientists at each location monitor the varieties. Samples are taken from ones that show signs of susceptibility, and the samples are sent to the laboratory for identification of the pathogen. When results from the trap nurseries are compiled, movement of pathogens and changes in virulence can be noted. This information provides a warning of an incipient breakdown in the resistance of widely grown varieties, giving governments perhaps 2 or 3 years in which to replace the susceptible varieties before an epidemic can develop.

Wheat technology laboratory

Industrialized countries use complex laboratory tests to measure wheat quality because the domestic milling industry and the export market demand precise wheat classifications. In most developing countries, however, two simple measurements are often sufficient: the weight of 1000 kernels and the weight of 1 hectoliter (100 liters) of grain. The first is an indicator of plumpness; the second, an indicator of grain density and flour yield.

Tests of grain color are needless because color is related to

Researchers use a light table to cull shriveled grains from the seeds to be used in the next generation of testing. (*Source:* CIMMYT.)

neither nutritional quality nor milling and baking qualities. Although tests for protein content provide an indication of quality for leavened bread, they serve less purpose in countries that consume unleavened wheat products such as flat breads or chapaties.

Usually a country is wise to concentrate its resources first on raising the quantity of wheat harvested. When the food supply is secure, resources can be devoted to raising quality. Mexico, for example, had no modern cereal technology laboratory until 1958, 2 years after reaching self-sufficiency in wheat production.

Plant quarantine service

A plant quarantine service is a supporting activity for problem-oriented research. It guards against importing alien diseases, insects, and weeds. When a country is importing seed of new varieties and lines for testing, a proper quarantine procedure is to require that a sanitary certificate issued by a competent authority accompany each importation of seed.

Unfortunately the quarantine services in some countries are burdened with complicated procedures copied from those of industrialized countries or left over from colonial administrations, and they are sometimes managed by officials who succeed primarily in delaying the introduction of modern germ plasm. Such procedures are more an obstacle than a help to development. Some countries import shiploads of food grains without quarantine precautions, thus risking the spread of pathogens from grain spilled from railroad cars and trucks, yet they impose excessive restrictions on packets of seed arriving from competent scientific agencies.

Decisions to admit or exclude seed should be based upon a reasonable weighing of the benefits to be gained and the risks involved. There is no such thing as zero biological risk.

Availability of inputs

The availability of agricultural inputs such as seeds, fertilizers, irrigation, and pesticides depends heavily on government investment or assistance.

Seed services

Seed supply is often the weak link in a wheat improvement program. Development of new varieties tends to run ahead of the multiplication and marketing of seed. Paradoxically a seed program for a self-pollinated plant like wheat should be a simple process. On one occasion in Mexico, seed of a wheat variety was multiplied from 200 grams to 100 tons within 12 months (see Chapter 3).

Among the common failings of seed programs is ignorance of farmers' needs. Farmers expect a seed program to produce seed that has somewhat better quality than the seed they save themselves or get from a neighbor. That means the seed should have a reasonable level of varietal purity, good germination, and low contamination from weed seed. Farmers also want to be able to get the seed within 1 or 2 years after the release of a new variety, not 8 or 10 years later as happens in many countries. Finally, farmers want seed available at a reasonable distance from their farms, not at a far-off government office.

The most widespread cause of ineffective seed programs is

the belief of government officials that civil servants can produce adequate seed on governmental farms and that seed can be marketed efficiently through a government agency. There are few instances of satisfactory results from this approach.

Seed programs run by government bureaucrats tend to be saddled with an inadequately trained staff, which is unable to grow a uniform crop. This problem stems in part from complicated employment procedures in government, which make it difficult to reward the best seed operators and to remove incompetent staff members.

When substandard seed is produced on a government farm, civil servants are timid about rejecting it. Instead they pass the poor product on to farmers. Seed is often sold too cheaply or below cost. Consequently the seed program depends on scarce government funds, which makes it difficult to erect proper storage buildings, to advertise the seed, or to pay for the travel of salesmen.

Successful seed programs have at least a degree of autonomy from the government bureaucracy, though they may be organized as government corporations. Control of these organizations is in the hands of boards of directors that include farmers and other members of the public. Seed production is separated from storage and marketing. To produce seed, successful programs contract with farmers and pay enough to provide an incentive for quality. Sales agents, organized down to the village level, likewise are given financial rewards for good work.

Some shortcomings of seed programs are the result of overly sophisticated seed standards in legislation, introduced by international seed specialists. Some systems recommended to governments have been developed in industrialized countries, but when the systems are transferred without adaptation to developing countries, they fail for lack of management skills and motivation. The elements of a sound program are discussed in *Successful seed programs* by Johnson E. Douglas.

Fertilizer stocks

Fertilizer is a driving force in the wheat revolution. In an unpublished study, the economist Per Pinstrup-Andersen found that 54 percent of the increased grain yields in developing countries between 1948 and 1973 could be credited to rising fertilizer use. In the late 1970s, developing countries applied an average of 28 kilograms of chemical nutrients to each crop hectare, a fourfold increase over 1964. But that rate still was only 20 percent of the amount used in Europe and North America.

The response of a wheat plant to nitrogen fertilizer differs among varieties, and it is also affected by the previous fertility of the soil. But a general principle can be stated: The first kilogram of nitrogen applied to a management-responsive wheat variety properly grown will produce — with sufficient moisture — about 20 kilograms of added grain. In very favorable environments, even 30 kilograms of grain may be added for each kilogram of nitrogen, up to the first 50 kilograms. The ratio of increased grain to added fertilizer starts to diminish at some application level between 50 and 100 kilograms of nitrogen. Eventually the fertilizer response curve levels off, and if the crop lodges, it declines.

Of course not all fertilizers are appropriate for all soils and crop needs. The fertilizer formula that can most economically correct a soil's deficiencies must be determined by local trials, and then appropriate fertilizer formulations must be made available to each wheat-growing region well before sowing time.

Chemical fertilizer will remain one of the essential elements of successful wheat programs even if petroleum prices continue to rise. Some governments keep the price ratio between nutrient nitrogen and wheat grain at 3.0 or less to encourage fertilizer use. (At that ratio, a farmer will apply fertilizer up to the approximate point where for each unit of money spent on fertilizer, he gets back three units of money from the additional grain produced. This relationship can reasonably apply only to the first 50 to 70 kilograms of nitrogen applied.)

Irrigation

Insufficient water is the main barrier to higher food production. The average yield of wheat grown under irrigation is double that of rainfed wheat. Moreover the only developing countries whose wheat yields are above 2000 kg/ha — Mexico, Egypt, North Korea, and China — irrigate a large proportion of their wheat areas.

Irrigation combined with proper drainage can transform wastelands into productive tracts. India, Pakistan, and China have constructed extensive systems of dams and canals, but most countries have neglected water development, and many of them have food deficits. Even India, despite its 35 million hectares of irrigated land, has vast untapped water resources. Perhaps 80 percent of the river water in India and Bangladesh flows into the sea unused.

Large capital investments in irrigation projects in developing countries have all too often been planned piecemeal. The objectives have typically been limited to huge dams, a network of irrigation canals, and, sometimes, hydroelectric generators. In most of these big projects, two essentials have been ignored. One is erosion control through proper management of forest cover and grasslands in the dam's watershed. Without erosion control, silting can easily cut the life of a reservoir in half. The second essential is a network of drainage canals to carry off the tailwater from irrigation. Without drainage, the water table rises, which brings salts into the root zone of the crops, reduces fertilizer response, depresses yields, and eventually, when the land becomes waterlogged, makes it unfit for crops. Millions of hectares of cropland have been abandoned for this reason.

Countries that have built huge irrigation systems without anticipating silted reservoirs or salted and waterlogged land need remedies. Erosion can be prevented above dams by planting trees and grass on the watersheds and instituting programs of controlled tree cutting and controlled grazing. Installing drainage canals will reduce salinity and improve crop yields.

When large irrigation projects are planned, they should draw on the skills of foresters and soil conservation experts for the watershed; hydraulic engineers for the dam, canals, and drains; hydroelectric engineers for the generators; industrial engineers for the fertilizer factories; agronomists and other crop scientists for the agricultural pattern; and economists to analyze the economic feasibility of the whole project. That kind of planning should lead to a more cost-effective system of water development in the future.

Pesticides

Weeds, diseases, insects, birds, and rodents annually reduce food-crop production in developing countries by an estimated 35 percent. For wheat, losses are estimated at 15 to 20 percent. Since World War II, there has been increasing dependence throughout the world on chemical pesticides. In general, the more developed a country, the greater its use of pesticides. For small farmers (2 hectares or less), suitable practices are only now being developed.

On wheat, herbicide has proved to be the most cost-effective

A scientist collects rust spores with a suction appliance to use in artificially inoculating wheat plants with rust. (*Source:* CIMMYT.)

and widely used pesticide. Although insects are less of a problem on wheat than on most other food crops, countries that suffer insect attacks on wheat are making effective use of insecticides. Fungicides are not commonly used, but Mexico employed fungicides to control an epidemic of leaf rust in 1977 (see Chapter 3).

The best way to prevent losses is to develop wheat varieties that are resistant to diseases and insects. But where resistant varieties are not yet available, or where varietal resistance has broken down and the crop is threatened, officials have a responsibility to understand the potential uses of pesticides, to facilitate their procurement where justified, and to ensure that they will be safely applied by supporting research trials and properly training extension workers.

Farm implements and traction

More than half the wheat in developing countries is produced with animal power (cattle, mules, horses, and camels). The spread of semi-dwarf wheats has required little change in production equipment except for seeding and threshing.

The seed for semi-dwarf wheats should be planted no more than 5 centimeters deep, but the bullock plow traditionally used in Asia covers the wheat seed with 10 to 15 centimeters of soil. Nevertheless farmers have found ways to adjust the wooden plow in order to leave the seed at the right depth. Hand-broadcasting methods can also be modified to remain effective for the new wheats. In many places, simple bullock-drawn or tractor-drawn implements that simultaneously drill seed and apply fertilizer have been manufactured locally.

Traditional ways of threshing wheat—for example, letting oxen trample it—become too slow when the yield doubles or triples. Some farmers have invested in motor-driven mechanical threshers, and as intensified cropping has demanded faster harvesting of wheat and planting of the succeeding crop, some farmers have purchased small tractors. The appropriate degree of mechanization needs to be determined by each farmer's circumstances.

Agricultural extension

Two myths are widely held about extension work. One is that the agent has a simple job and therefore should be paid less than other agricultural employees. The other is that the agent needs training only in "communications," that is, in organizing meetings, making speeches, and showing movies. Nothing is further from the truth. The extension agent should understand every problem on the farm. In this respect, the agent needs broader experience than the individual researcher.

Training the extension agent

Many extension workers feel insecure because they know less than the farmer about crop production. The remedy is production training—a course of supervised practice in growing a wheat crop. That practice is the core of the training for extension workers at international centers like CIMMYT. Such training is best supervised by researchers.

A few production agronomists trained at international research centers have been asked, after returning home, to set up training courses for extension workers. The trainer uses a local research station as a classroom so that the curriculum includes the latest research findings. On-farm demonstrations can be incorporated as an additional training device.

Two extension procedures can serve as training components. One is the use of the crop specialist to work with extension generalists. A wheat specialist may be assigned to assist every 20 to 25 generalists. Whenever a generalist encounters a wheat problem that is unfamiliar to him, he calls in the wheat specialist, and they visit the farmer's field together. Wheat specialists might be borrowed from a university faculty or from the research service.

Another procedure has been called the "training-and-visit system." Before the planting season, the extension supervisor and a research specialist meet with the extension agents for 2 weeks to demonstrate land preparation, seeding, and fertilizer application and to determine what to demonstrate to farmers. Classwork is then suspended for 2 weeks while the extension agents visit their assigned farmers. When the agents return to the classroom, they discuss weed control; then go back to the farmers for 2 weeks, and so on through irrigation, threshing, farm storage, and marketing of wheat. Pakistan successfully used this procedure during the introduction of short wheats in the 1960s.

Extension transportation

An extension agent must be able to reach farms easily. Transportation is the costliest element in an extension program, but there is no substitute if agents are to maintain contact with farmers. A practical arrangement is to have most agents live in the villages they serve and move about by bicycle. Their supervisor gets a motorcycle, and the district director of extension is provided with a light truck.

On-farm demonstrations, field days, and contests

Effective extension services place hundreds of demonstrations in farmers' fields, and demonstrations become the chief activity of the extension agent during the wheat season. A typical demonstration might cover a quarter or a half hectare and contain two wheat varieties, one widely used and one newly released, grown under two levels of fertilizer and with two methods of weed control. The demonstration should be simple and result in easily recognized differences. If yields are increased only 5 or 10 percent, the results may be confused with weather effects, but if yields rise 50 or 100 percent, the lesson is persuasive.

Field days should be held at harvesttime for farmers in the vicinity of the demonstration sites. Cutting and weighing part of the crop during the field day will make the results more dramatic. Agricultural universites may participate in the field days or hold separate harvest events.

A related extension technique is the national yield contest, with prizes offered to farmers who achieve the highest yields. Here again field days—with crop cutting and weighing before the crowd—provide impressive proof of what modern varieties can accomplish if combined with sound agronomic practices. The world's highest cereal yields—of wheat, maize, barley, rice, sorghum, and millet—have all been achieved in this type of farmer contest, which attracts wide publicity. India created a "1-ton club" for wheat farmers, giving national recognition to anyone who achieved a commercial wheat yield of 2000 pounds per acre (2250 kg/ha).

Maximizing extension contacts

There are many ways to increase the number of farmers each agent can assist. An agent could participate in meetings of local farmers' associations or cooperatives, so he can present his message to 50 or 100 farmers at a time rather than dealing with them one by one. Another technique is the system of "model farmers" developed in Bangladesh at Comilla Academy. The model farmers are progressive individuals who attend weekly meetings to discuss current farm activities. Then they return to their villages and pass on the lessons through a meeting of their neighbors. The model farmer may be a volunteer or receive part-time pay.

Extraneous assignments

Agricultural extension workers are sometimes rendered ineffective because they are assigned extraneous duties. Some are required to be loan collectors for the credit programs. Some serve as tax assessors. Some are family-planning agents. These assignments reduce extension workers' credibility and lead to a conflict of interest. The extension service suffers.

Maintaining staff morale

Extension workers in developing countries often have less education and lower salaries than researchers, and this situation affects morale. Some governments improve morale by giving public recognition to top achievers. When national leaders visit the countryside, they ask to be accompanied by the local extension agent and indicate in their talks with farmers that the extension worker is a valued public employee. The national honors list, traditional in some countries, should include superior extension workers among the people decorated.

When the substandard pay for extension agents is caused by an excessive number of employees, it would be better to reduce the staff and provide adequate pay for those retained.

Economic policies

The sources of financial support for a wheat program are commonly scattered among various government bodies: the ministry of finance, the ministry of agriculture, the central bank, the planning commission, and sometimes the office of the prime minister. As a result a wheat-program administrator is not his own master. Ways must be found to persuade other officials to approve financial policies that will stimulate wheat production. To do this, the administrator must be familiar with a variety of financial areas.

Farm credit

Modern agriculture always requires production credit. The credit system comprises private commercial banks, farmers' associations, cooperatives, and various government loan agencies. Their agricultural lending activities are usually backed by guarantees from the central bank. Credit systems tend to meet the needs of the progressive, better-educated farmers first, and to have difficulty in accommodating small farmers who have limited resources.

Small borrowers can be divided into two categories. One is people with so few resources that they cannot support their families even at subsistence levels. These borrowers cannot solve their needs with agricultural credit. They require income from off-farm employment, preferably from the development of rural industries This development is the role of a small-industries bank or corporation. China, India, and South Korea are examples of countries that have had success in rural small-industry development.

The second category consists of farmers whose resources, if properly used, can produce a surplus of crops for sale but who lack the working capital to switch from traditional methods to modern agricultural practices. These small borrowers deserve serious attention from lending agencies, because only with increased working capital will they be able to afford the higher input cost of the new wheat technology.

Agencies serving small farmers have stressed four requirements for success. First, loans should be made available on a schedule that immediately precedes the farmer's expenditures. Second, loans should be made in kind (that is, in seed, fertilizer, etc.), but the farmer should be permitted to choose the inputs he wants. Third, repayment should be deferred if the farmer suffers a weather calamity. Fourth, credit agencies should have sufficient staff to deal with large numbers of small farmers, thus reducing each farmer's paperwork.

Rural banks that have added extra personnel to supervise small loans have experienced a higher repayment rate than those that copied their staffing patterns from urban banks, which give larger loans and have fewer supervising officers.

Price supports for wheat

Most wheat-producing countries set a minimum guaranteed price for wheat. The guarantee is intended to encourage farmers to plant wheat and to use modern inputs (good seed, adequate fertilizer, and pesticides, where appropriate). To be an incentive, the guaranteed price level must be announced 1 or 2 months before planting time, and countries that are experiencing severe inflation require some formula for adjustment of the price supports. The government must then be prepared to buy wheat from the farmers if the open market price after harvest falls below the guaranteed price. To do so, the government must have storage facilities. Most developing countries set the guaranteed price approximately equal to the landed cost of imported wheat. If the guaranteed price is much higher or lower than the world price, it encourages smuggling.

Farm input subsidies

Many governments subsidize farm inputs. In few places do farmers pay the full cost for irrigation water, fertilizer, or improved seed. Some governments even provide pesticides, farm machinery, or electricity for irrigation pumps at less than cost. Three arguments for input subsidies are put forward by supporters of this policy: (1) The farmer who can buy inputs cheaply is more likely to use them than a farmer who only receives a guaranteed price for his wheat; (2) subsidized inputs do not raise the consumer price of wheat whereas a guaranteed price to the farmer is passed on to consumers, including the urban poor; and (3) input subsidies can be tailored to different regions, based on development level, and to individuals, based on the size of operation.

Input subsidies also have flaws. For example, fertilizer that is subsidized to benefit food crops is sometimes transferred to industrial crops like cotton, tobacco, or sugar. Nevertheless, subsidized inputs remain a reasonably efficient tool by which the wheat administrator can manipulate greater production.

Wheat imports

Four out of five developing countries were steady importers of wheat during the 1970s. This flow of foreign grain often undercuts campaigns to increase local wheat production. When imported wheat is sold to developing countries at concessional prices, it offers unfair competition to local wheat. Moreover, imported wheat arrives in large shipments (10,000 tons or more) and has uniform quality; hence local millers find it easier to handle than the local wheat, which is usually not uniform in quality and requires greater management efforts to accumulate 10,000 tons at the mill.

An administrator concerned with domestic wheat production will need to negotiate with other government officials and convince them to establish policies on foreign grain deliveries and prices that minimize injury to local farmers.

Food subsidies

"Fair price shops" are operated by a government food agency in many countries. These shops generally handle only basic foodstuffs, and their purpose is to hold down the cost of living for the lower-income classes. The shops enable the government to purchase products from the rural producer at the prevailing farm price and to sell to a restricted public at a lower price, the difference being absorbed by the government as a social subsidy.

A policy of food subsidies is not a flexible policy. Once started, it is politically difficult to change the system or even to reduce the level of subsidy.

Budgeting for the wheat-production program

How much to budget for research and extension work is a difficult question for the administrator. In *National and international agricultural research and extension programs*, Boyce and Evenson reported surveying more than 100 countries to determine public expenditures on research and extension during 1959 to 1974, and they compared the budgets with the gross agricultural product of each country. They found that in 1974 industrialized countries spent a little over 2 percent of their gross agricultural product on agricultural research and 0.56 percent on extension. Developing countries in the same year were spending a somewhat smaller percentage on research and 0.9 to 2.2 percent on extension. The authors comment: "many low-income countries appear to believe that it is possible to substitute large quantities of low-priced extension resources for the relatively high-priced research resources. . . . It has not, in practice, been a wise course of action to pursue an aggressive extension program while neglecting the difficult task of building research capabilities" (p. 47).

Dealing with an oversupply of wheat

A country that aims for self-sufficiency in wheat must prepare for an oversupply because once an improved and profitable technology is introduced, farmers are likely to surpass the production targets. It is worthwhile for an administrator of an accelerated wheat program to become familiar with ways of dealing with abundance.

Food reserves and grain storage

Most developing countries maintain a food reserve, which requires storage facilities. In most countries, legislative bodies are slow to invest in grain storage facilities until a crisis looms. When India's grain reserves reached 22 million tons in 1978, only 9 million tons of grain could be stored under weatherproof conditions. The balance was in temporary facilities and faced greater risk. When Turkey's wheat stockpile reached 5 million tons in the late 1970s, more than half was stored on the ground under plastic covers. Such an arrangement is feasible only in areas of low rainfall and extreme temperatures, as severe cold in winter and intense dry heat in summer help control insects that infest stored grain. Turkey's emergency storage method was usable on the Anatolian plateau, but not in the lowlands where higher rainfall prevails. Turkey and India were fortunate to escape with minimum storage losses. India now plans a substantial expansion of its permanent grain storage facilities, a decision that can be recommended to any wheat-surplus country in a high-rainfall, high-humidity area.

Wheat export opportunities

Few developing countries have been successful in penetrating the highly competitive world wheat-export market. Costs of production in developing countries tend to be above the world export price. Their transportation and port facilities usually are inadequate, and their wheat tends to be nonuniform in quality and contaminated with stones, weed seeds, and chaff. Of the developing countries, only Argentina has historically been a large exporter, but in recent years, India and Turkey have exported significant quantities of wheat. Aside from shipments to neighbors, it is unlikely that other developing countries will soon join the exporters' club, with the possible exception of Pakistan.

Feed uses of wheat

Wheat can be a valuable ingredient of feeds for milk cows, beef cattle, poultry, and swine. Wheat has a higher nutritional value than the major feed grains such as maize, sorghum, and barley, but wheat is normally higher priced as well. In developing countries, whole-grain wheat is usually fed to animals only when the grain has sprouted, shriveled, or been frost damaged.

Millfeeds (the by-products of wheat milling) are a valuable raw material for mixed animal feeds. Of the wheat grain that enters a mill, 26 to 28 percent, by weight, comes out as millfeeds. The rest is flour. The millfeed percentage is lower in some developing countries because millers seek to maximize the output of flour for human consumption. Millfeeds vary in nutritional value, but typically they contain 13 to 14 percent protein (higher than whole wheat), 2.5 to 3.0 percent fat (also higher than whole wheat), and 9 to 12 percent fiber, which is of feeding value only for ruminants.

Because of their high oil content, millfeeds are vulnerable to more severe losses in storage than is whole grain. They must be safeguarded against the molds induced by excess moisture, as well as against birds, rodents, and insects. In a country like India, where millfeeds from flour milling are measured in millions of tons, these by-products require careful attention from the administrators of the national food supply. In China, millfeeds from wheat and rice play a major role in the huge production of swine.

Industrial uses of wheat

Wheat is a good raw material for industrial starch (sizing for paper), for adhesives in making plywood, and for industrial alcohol. But little wheat is used for these purposes because other agricultural products such as maize cost less. During World War II, the United States converted 3 million tons of wheat a year to industrial alcohol, which was in demand for making explosives. After the war, this usage dropped virtually to nil. In recent years, gasohol, a mixture of gasoline and ethyl alcohol, has been produced as a fuel for vehicles, but sugarcane, maize, and cassava have proved to be cheaper raw materials than wheat for making alcohol.

Food-for-work programs

China and India have demonstrated ways to use a grain supply as capital for financing rural public works such as irrigation and drainage structures, farm-to-market roads, reforestation, and schools. The concept sounds simple, but the mobilization problems are enormous: A rural population that is idle in the winter season is paid with grain to serve in a massive labor force to construct improvements in the agricultural resource base, which will further increase the productivity of agriculture. In the late 1970s, India annually used up to 3 million tons of food grain for this purpose.

Promoting substitute crops for wheat

The administrator who is confronted with a persistent oversupply of wheat may fall back upon other crops to replace wheat. The crop substitutes will be chosen by local research trials and after a review of the local food demand. Likely candidates will come from groups such as winter oilseeds — like rapeseed — winter forage legumes or grasses, or winter green vegetables (a 60-day crop might be grown in autumn and again in early spring).

Farmers' service organizations

Progressive farmers' service organizations can help the administrator of a wheat program by supporting research, participating in extension work, producing and selling seed, managing irrigation systems, or serving as supply and marketing cooperatives. Among the outstanding examples are the Patronato in Mexico (see Chapter 3), the village associations of South Korea, and the irrigation societies and farmers' associations of Taiwan. These associations play an important role in identifying problems that require research and thus keep the research service relevant and accountable.

Psychological factors

Every wheat revolution has changed the attitudes of farmers, extension agents, research scientists, program administrators, and, ultimately, political leaders. Psychological factors cannot be ignored.

In countries where wheat revolutions have taken place, psychological change typically started with the research scientists, because they were the first to grow modern wheats with modern production methods. Some senior scientists initially were pessimistic. Some said they had tested wheats for a lifetime and did not believe that new technology could change their country's agriculture. They were hostile toward imported ideas. Some opposed interdisciplinary research because it broke up private domains. Some opposed wheat testing across climatic zones because it exposed scientists who had little competence with the crop. A few scientists had to be removed before a revolution could take off.

Next the psychological changes reached the extension agents. They too were often pessimistic. They said that agriculture had not changed in centuries and they were unable to get excited about new wheat varieties. They protested the volume of work involved in on-farm trials. They resisted close association with the research service because it upset the status quo.

Then psychological change reached the farmers. Many farmers were reluctant to collaborate with government officers whose recommendations had seldom proved useful. But to the surprise of many people, farmers proved flexible. They were receptive when shown a technology that demonstrated a large increase in yield without a disproportionate increase in risk. Within a few years, farmers were visiting the research stations and asking about the latest developments.

The new attitudes among farmers affected government administrators at an early stage of the wheat revolution. The demand for improved seed, fertilizer, and herbicides, rising from thousands of newly persuaded farmers, put pressure on many administrators and political leaders.

Successful administrators acquired the enthusiasm of football coaches. They were able to instill confidence in their agricultural team. They developed an understanding of all elements of the program. They insisted on new forms of cooperation between research and extension, ending their separation into two camps.

The minister of agriculture and chief of state were sometimes the last to shift attitudes. On field trips, they heard talk of radical new developments affecting wheat. They inquired. They saw the political significance. Then the shrewd ones took over the leadership. In one Asian country, the chief of state, explaining his role to a visitor, tapped his finger on the telephone and said: "Here is the most powerful element in the wheat revolution. When I hear that some staff member is lagging, I pick up the telephone and call the officer involved. He promises action, but I tell him, 'I don't want promises; I want your return telephone call by tomorrow telling me what you have accomplished.'"

A wheat revolution develops its own style, and this is nowhere more distinctive than in the psychological factor, which rests ultimately with the program administrator.

The dynamic program leader

No element of a wheat program is more critical than its leadership. The program leader is the field commander, serving under direction of the staff officers in his ministry. This program leader most often is a trained agricultural scientist who first established his excellence in his own branch of science, then rose to a supervisory post, from which he broadened his understanding of other aspects of crop production. The qualified leader is able to inspire superior work from those around him and below him. He is not afraid of the unknown. He shows vision. He senses when to move the program cautiously and when to call for aggressive all-out action. He is able to arouse team spirit. He communicates a sense of excitement to his superiors—from the minister of agriculture up to the chief of state—and receives full support from them in return. It is this shared enthusiasm that has brought success to a few national wheat programs. It is the distinguishing accomplishment of the dynamic program leader.

Postharvest Wheat Handling

The farmer's risk does not end when the crop is mature. Grain may be lost during harvest because of shattering and spillage, or birds, rodents, and insects may consume it in the field or in storage. Furthermore, the value of the harvested grain may be reduced by contamination with earth, stones, weed seeds, and animal droppings or by invasion of mold. Mold may make the grain inedible or even toxic. Postharvest grain losses in some countries have been estimated at 10 to 15 percent of production and higher.

People responsible for wheat production programs need to be acquainted with the steps of postharvest technology and ways to prevent losses.

Harvesting and threshing

In Asia, which produces most of the developing world's wheat, perhaps 80 percent of the wheat farmers cut the crop by hand with a sickle or scythe. The sheaves of wheat are carried to the threshing area and spread out to dry in the sun and wind for a day or more. Threshing — separation of the kernels from the stems — is done in a variety of ways. The wheat may be beaten with flails or trampled by humans or animals. Animals may be used to draw a stone roller over the wheat, or a similar implement consisting of a series of steel disks may be used. In some places, a small tractor may be repeatedly driven over the wheat.

After threshing, the straw is stacked around the threshing area; later it may be used as animal feed or bedding, as cooking fuel, as a component in sun-dried bricks, or in compost. The wheat kernels — still intermixed with pieces of straw, chaff, broken grains, stones, and dirt — are spread on the threshing floor for further drying.

A "plot" thresher being used at a research station in Turkey. Such small threshers facilitate measuring the harvest from experimental plots. (*Source:* Bill Wright.)

Various labor-saving devices are employed in some farming communities. An old and simple improvement in threshing, which is used by some farmers, is to grasp a sheaf of wheat and beat the grain heads against a low wall, an oil drum, or a wagon bed. This method is more efficient than trampling because the kernels fall into a container or onto a woven mat and thus are less likely to become contaminated.

Pedal- or motor-driven mechanical threshers have been devised to save labor. One type has a revolving drum with projecting teeth that strip off the kernels when a sheaf of wheat is held against the moving surface. The tractor-drawn combine and self-propelled harvester cause the least contamination, but they require the largest capital investment. Some threshers have now been designed for use by farmers who cultivate only 1 or 2 hectares. These machines are light enough to be carried from one field to another by two people.

The most critical decision in harvesting is not the degree of mechanization but the timing. If the harvest starts late, the grain becomes too dry, which increases the amount of grain that shatters and falls to the ground. The longer a ripe crop stands in the field, the higher the chances of loss from hailstones, fire, birds, or rodents. On the other hand, if the harvest starts too early, the moisture content of the grain is high, and drying will be difficult.

Cleaning

After threshing, the straw, chaff, immature grains, sand, stones, and other foreign matter should be separated from the grain. In traditional hand winnowing, a shallow basket containing grain is held overhead, and the grain is tossed into the wind. Broken grain, straw, and weed seeds, being lighter, are carried by the wind to one side, and the whole grain falls to the feet of the winnower. The winnower may stand on a stool to give the falling grain longer exposure to the wind. Hand winnowing requires a brisk wind and must be repeated many times. Even then, the results are erratic, and the grain is far from clean.

Simple, low-cost appliances that use hand-driven or motorized blowers and are more efficient and less time-consuming than hand winnowing have been developed. An FAO publication, *Processing and storage of foodgrains by rural families*, describes grain cleaners that are suitable for village use. Large grain warehouses and flour mills need more-sophisticated grain cleaners; lending agencies that finance grain storage facilities can provide advice on the appropriate cleaning equipment for them.

Drying

The moisture content of wheat grain is a critical factor from harvest until milling. Although a moisture content of 25 percent is not uncommon in newly harvested grain, it must be dried to 14 percent immediately to protect it against mold. At 14 percent moisture, the grain can be safely held for 2 to 3 months. If it is to be stored for longer periods, say 4 to 12 months, the moisture content must be reduced to 13 percent or less.

Drying in many wheat-growing countries of Asia, Africa, and Latin America is done by spreading a thin layer of grain in the sun — sometimes on the threshing floor, sometimes on rooftops, sometimes on highway pavements. Sun drying is risky because it depends on the weather and it leads to dirty grain.

Few small farmers can individually afford mechanical equipment for cleaning and drying, but they could cooperatively own equipment. Some commercial grain buyers or government warehouses offer to accumulate the grain of small farmers, bulk it, and clean and dry it with modern equipment. Unfortunately such a service is rare in developing countries.

Marketing

Half to three fourths of the wheat produced in developing countries does not enter marketing channels. It is consumed by the families who grow it, though they may periodically bring a sack of wheat to town for grinding at a small mill and carry the flour back home for family use.

The rest of the wheat (25 to 50 percent of production) is sold by the farmers to a local grain merchant or to a government agency. This wheat enters the marketing process: storage for a few months to a year, followed by milling into flour at an industrial mill, then distribution to commercial bakeries or to foodshops where the urban consumer buys flour for home baking.

The wheat most farmers produce is unlikely to reach the export market. Developing countries export only 5 million to 7 million tons per year, nearly all of which originates in just three countries — Argentina, Turkey, and India. On the other hand, in recent years, 40 million to 50 million tons of wheat a year were imported by over 100 developing countries. The handling and marketing of imported wheat is little different from the handling and marketing of locally produced wheat.

Handling and transporting

Traditional labor-intensive systems of grain movement serve to minimize capital investment in countries where the cost of labor is low in relation to the cost of capital. But the more times wheat is loaded and unloaded from wagons, trucks, railroad cars, and barges between farm and mill, the greater the losses and the higher the costs. In some developing countries, bagged wheat may be loaded on vehicles and unloaded by hand up to 20 times before it is milled. By contrast, there are highly efficient handling systems in which loose wheat is loaded into trucks by an auger, moved to the grain processing center in a single trip, dumped into a receiving bin by gravity, and moved by mechanical conveyor through the cleaning and drying processes and into storage; it is then moved out of storage into the flour mill, at the same location, where the finished flour is mechanically bagged, loaded into trucks by elevator, and taken to the commercial bakery or the retail market without once being handled on the backs of laborers. National policy regarding the appropriate degree of mechanical wheat handling is often based on the need to maximize employment for unskilled labor.

Storage

The wheat harvest lasts only a few months, but consumption continues year around, hence the need for storage facilities. Some of the wheat that farm families hold for their own use is piled in farm buildings without proper flooring and with open doors and windows, so it is subject to losses caused by molds, birds, rodents, and insects. These losses can be essentially eliminated by using low-cost storage facilities that can be constructed from local materials. Many families in Bangladesh use efficient storage containers of sun-dried mud; in China, work brigades have constructed bamboo-and-mud silos that hold 8000 kilograms of grain. The FAO has prepared illustrated publications on low-cost structures for storing grain.

The wheat that moves off the farm at harvest to the village merchant or to a government food corporation presents a different set of storage problems. This wheat may be kept in large steel bins, in concrete silos, or in the holding bins of a flour mill (mills need to be able to hold sufficient grain for 30 to 60 days of milling). Or wheat may be temporarily stored in railroad cars or in open piles in market towns where protection is little better than on a village threshing floor.

Protecting grain in storage

The threats to stored grain are birds, rodents, insects, moisture, and fungi. For birds and rodents, the best defense is to keep them out. Bird-proofing involves placing wire screens over openings under the eaves of storage buildings and over windows and doors

Miniloaves made from experimental wheat being tested in a baking laboratory. (*Source:* CIMMYT.)

that are left open. Making a building rodent-proof requires concrete floors and metal shields around the doors and windows.

Thirteen species of insects that feed on grain are adapted to the storage environment. Two species of weevil will attack whole kernels of grain. Other species of grain insects (beetles and the larval stages of some moths) feed mainly on grain dust and broken kernels. The food value of stored grain can quickly deteriorate when conditions are favorable for insects to multiply. In large numbers, storage pests induce the development of molds, which lead to heating (up to 40°C), which damages the grain.

Fumigation is the most practical way to control insects in grain. (However, fumigation practices appropriate for grain to be used for food are risky in grain intended for seed because excessive fumigation can reduce germination disastrously.) Fortunately, with proper control measures, wheat can be stored for years without appreciable insect or mold damage.

Fungi cause the greatest losses in stored wheat. "Sick wheat" is the term applied to stored grain that has been invaded by fungi. The mold caused by fungi damages wheat in several ways. It gives the grain a musty odor, discolors the germ, and lowers flour yield and baking quality. In seed, the heat of spoilage reduces germination. Sometimes mold may make the grain unfit for human or livestock consumption.

Such fungi as *Fusarium, Helminthosporium,* and *Alternaria,* which infect wheat grains as they develop in the field, do not continue to grow in stored grain, because the moisture content is usually too low (but they remain viable). Thus, after harvest, the grain is invaded by storage fungi, the spores of which are always present around stored grain. Since the spores cannot be eliminated, control measures consist of preventing the spores from germinating and growing.

The ability of spores to germinate is determined by the moisture content of the grain, the temperature of the grain, and the length of time in storage. When the moisture content of the grain is below 13 percent, storage fungi will not grow, no matter how long the grain is stored. At moisture levels above 13 percent, growth of fungi increases with temperature: At 5° to 15°C, fungi grow very slowly; at 30° to 40°C, they grow rapidly. Length of storage is an added factor. Grain stored for a few weeks before being milled into flour can be safely kept at a somewhat higher moisture content and temperature than grain that is stored for months or years.

The moisture content of stored wheat is much more difficult to control than insects. In modern bulk storage facilities, a stream of air is continuously forced through the grain, which reduces both the moisture content and the temperature. The farm family can achieve the same results by emptying its storage bin periodically and spreading the grain in the sun. The process is very time-consuming, however.

Storage methods

Several countries have succeeded in controlling stored grain losses. China has been exceptional in combining three systems of storage: in the household, in village silos, and in government warehouses.

Families in the wheat-growing areas of China store grain in thick pottery jars about 1 meter high and 1 meter in diameter. The jars are covered with plastic or pottery lids held in place by weights. Each jar holds about 400 kilograms of grain, so three jars will hold the yearly grain supply for a family of four. The jars are kept in a living room or bedroom where signs of insects or molds are easily noticed so countermeasures can be taken when needed.

Village reserves of wheat are stored in silos, each 3 meters high and 3 meters in diameter with a cone-shaped roof. The silos are made by erecting a bamboo frame, plastering it with mud outside and inside, and sealing the structure with a coating of cow dung and whitewash. Sometimes a plastic sheet lines the inside of the silo. An opening at the top permits the loading of grain, and an opening at the bottom permits unloading. The openings are sealed with transparent plastic. The capacity of each silo is about 8000 kilograms. Most "work brigades" in North China have a row of these silos standing beside a village road. Grain losses are avoided by drying the grain properly before loading, by using fumigants, and by frequent inspection.

The central government stores its grain reserve in concrete buildings, which commonly hold 25,000 tons. The buildings are near railroad junctions and adjacent to flour mills. In the warehouse, loose grain is heaped on waterproof concrete floors with sheets of plastic separating the grain from the walls. Flour is stored in sacks. Grain reserves are held near the production center, and only the milled flour is shipped to cities, which reduces the transport weight by 25 to 30 percent. Millfeeds are fed to animals raised near the mill.

Other countries have devised effective storage structures made from indigenous materials. India has an experimental grain storage center in Uttar Pradesh where many types of drying and storage methods are on display. Some storage structures, when sealed tight, will prevent insect damage since the carbon dioxide generated by the grain suppresses insect development.

On the Anatolian plateau of Turkey, a low-cost method of temporary storage has been developed. Grain is stored in long piles on plastic sheets placed on sloping ground, which provides drainage. The piles are covered with heavy plastic sheets and topped with soil to shut out moisture. The system works because the grain is thoroughly dried in the sun before storage and because the hot, dry summers and cold winters suppress insects that infest stored grain.

Milling and grading

A whole kernel of wheat consists of four main parts: the outer covering or seedcoat, which is approximately 10 percent of the kernel's weight; the aleurone layer under the seedcoat, which is 6 percent of the weight; the endosperm (starchy middle), which is 81 percent of the weight; and the germ, which is 3 percent of the weight.

Grinding or milling wheat yields two primary products—flour and millfeeds. In preparation for milling, the grain is cleaned, and then the moisture content of the grain is increased to facilitate separating the bran (the outer portion of the kernel plus the aleurone layer) and the germ from the starchy interior (endosperm). The milling process generally yields 72 to 74 percent flour. The rest is millfeeds. The proportion of flour can be raised if necessary, such as when a country is trying to minimize wheat imports. If only the coarsest bran is removed to produce whole wheat flour, recovery runs as high as 90 percent. Attaining the theoretical maximum yield of white flour, 81 percent, is prevented by a deep crease that runs down one side of the seed. The roller milling process has been evolved to get the best possible separation of the endosperm from the bran.

Generally speaking, milling losses are highest in the older mills and lowest in the latest design of mills. But the "flour extraction rate" for different mill runs can vary considerably, depending on the way it is calculated: as a percentage of the wheat from which the flour is derived ("dirty wheat" as received at the mill, or "clean wheat" as fed to the rollers) or as a percentage of the total mill products, excluding the milling losses.

India and Pakistan have developed a small stone mill as a cottage industry. The mill grinds wheat into coarse flour (*atta*), removing only the coarsest bran. It is driven by a 1-horsepower motor and has eliminated the drudgery of hand pounding the grain in most villages.

Industrialized countries have systems for grading flours based upon texture, protein and ash content, and other physical and chemical measurements. Automated commercial bakeries demand detailed grading systems as they need precise and consistent flour characteristics for manufacturing wheat products. Such exacting standards are not necessary in most developing countries, although large bakeries in such cities as New Delhi, Cairo, Mexico City, and Buenos Aires seek standardized flours from local mills.

Commercial bakeries

As recently as World War II, more than half the wheat products of the United States were baked in the home, whereas by the

1970s, over 95 percent of wheat products were baked in commercial establishments. Such a shift is beginning in the developing countries. The proportion of bread, chapaties, tortillas, and other products that are produced by commercial enterprises is increasing rapidly.

Composite flour

Composite flour is hardly new. Since prehistoric times, bread in many European countries has been made from a mixture of wheat and rye flours. During the two world wars, bean flour, potato flour, and barley flour were commonly mixed with wheat flour for breadmaking.

As a taste for wheat products has grown in developing countries, increasing amounts of scarce foreign exchange have been spent on wheat imports. To reduce the need for importing wheat, many countries are testing mixtures of wheat flour with starch from maize, rice, or cassava or with flour from sorghum, millet, or triticale. Several organizations, including the Central Food Technology Research Institute in India, the FAO, and the Tropical Products Institute in the United Kingdom, have demonstrated that wheat flours mixed with 5 to 30 percent of substitute components can produce bakery products of acceptable appearance, flavor, and nutritional quality.

Wheat for feed and industrial use

Little wheat that is suitable for human consumption is fed to animals in developing countries because other feeds are less expensive. Likewise, little wheat is diverted to factory use, although wheat is a useful raw material for several industrial processes, including the manufacture of industrial starch and alcohol (see Chapter 7).

Promising Wheat Research
for the Future

What lines of research will do the most good for a country that has a limited budget and a small wheat staff? And what wheat research going on elsewhere is likely to produce improved technology suitable for the country? No single answer serves all countries. Many problems that affect individual countries are not worldwide in scope. Nonetheless there are several promising research approaches that could help all wheat growers achieve higher and more stable yields:

- Studies to reduce harvest fluctuations
- Studies to narrow the yield gap between the research station and farmers' fields, and between average farmers and the best farmers
- On-farm studies to learn more about the farmers' problems
- Studies in the research station to raise the yield potential

YIELD DEPENDABILITY

To ensure steadier wheat production, scientists must develop varieties that have reliable disease resistance and greater tolerance to environmental stress. Diseases reduce wheat yields worldwide by perhaps 15 to 20 percent, which suggests that the loss to developing countries is 20 million to 30 million tons annually. Of course disease incidence rises and falls, causing wide fluctuations in harvests from year to year.

Nine fungus diseases of wheat cause significant losses (see Table 10), and there are more than 30 less-damaging diseases. If a susceptible wheat variety is grown in an area where one of the

Table 10
Major fungus diseases of bread wheat in developing countries (estimates by CIMMYT)

Common name and pathogen	Yield loss, susceptible varieties (%)		Endemic areas as a proportion of total wheat area (%)	Hot spots—areas where disease is most severe
	Average, in endemic area	In epidemic		
Stem rust *Puccinia graminis* f. sp. *tritici*	40	up to 100	50	Highlands of Kenya and Ethiopia; Parana State, Brazil; South India
Leaf rust *Puccinia recondita* f. sp. *tritici*	15–20	up to 50	90	Mexico, India, Pakistan, Bangladesh, China
Stripe rust *Puccinia striiformis* f. sp. *tritici*	40	up to 100	33	Highlands of South America and East Africa; North Africa; Mideast; Indo-Gangetic Plain of India and Pakistan
Septoria (leaf and glume blotch) *Septoria tritici* and *S. nodorum*	20–30	up to 100	20	Argentina, Brazil, Chile, Mediterranean coast, Ethiopia, Central America

Disease				
Scab (head blight) *Fusarium* spp.	10–15	50–100	30–40	China, Argentina, Brazil
Helminthosporium (common root rot, seedling blight, leaf blight) *Helminthosporium sativum*	5–10	up to 100	10–15	Eastern India, Nepal, Bangladesh, Zambia
Powdery mildew *Erysiphe graminis* f. sp. *tritici*	30	up to 100	10	China, Chile, Iran, Mediterranean coast
Bunt *Tilletia* spp.	5–10	up to 50	10–15	Turkey, Mideast, Himalayan highlands of India and Pakistan
Loose smut *Ustilago tritici*	1–10	up to 30	30	Argentina, Indo-Gangetic Plain of India and Pakistan, Turkey, Mideast

serious fungus diseases is endemic, the crop will frequently suffer a severe reduction in yield.

Resistance to rusts

Rusts are the most destructive diseases of wheat. The fungi that cause rusts mutate readily, enabling them to rapidly develop new races (strains) that can attack wheat varieties that were resistant to the previously prevalent races. Rusts can spread far and fast because air currents carry spores long distances. The wheat breeder fights back by testing large numbers of wheat varieties to identify ones that have genetic resistance to a broad spectrum of the races of a fungus. Resistant varieties are then used in crosses to develop even greater concentrations of genes for disease resistance. Since the pathogens are constantly mutating and sometimes reproducing sexually, the creation and release of resistant varieties through dynamic breeding programs and competent seed multiplication is the most reliable safeguard against epidemics.

A type of resistance called "slow rusting" has recently been found, but it is not fully understood. Certain wheat varieties develop lesions—the symptoms of rust—but the lesions spread slowly until the plants are near maturity. Although at that time the full disease symptoms may become apparent, yield is not materially affected because the grain is already formed. Examples of "slow rusters" are the Mexican spring-wheat varieties Penjamo 62, Torim 73, and Pavon 76. CIMMYT is crossing "slow rusters" with high-yielding varieties to give a greater stability of resistance to the progeny.

Other weapons against rusts

Several new concepts for reducing the risk of rust are undergoing trial: multilines, varietal mixtures, and geographic placement of varieties. Each could become an important disease control mechanism.

Multilines

A multiline is a mechanical mixture of seeds from similar wheat types (that is, plants resembling each other in such characters as plant height, head type, maturity period, and grain appearance) but having different genes for rust resistance. The idea behind the multiline is to stabilize rust resistance and, hence, yield. When a new biotype of rust begins to attack the multiline, the chances are that only one or two components will be susceptible, so the disease will be unable to build to epidemic scale before the crop matures.

The multiline has been accepted by a few wheat breeders as a sound idea for minimizing the dangers of epidemics and stabilizing yields, but procedures for getting wheat multilines into commercial use still have to be developed (however, an oat multiline, developed for resistance to crown rust, has already been released in the United States).

CIMMYT has worked with several nations to develop multilines from cross 8156, from which such varieties as Siete Cerros in Mexico, Mexipak in Pakistan, and Kalyansona in India were selected. These varieties have been among the most successful in history, but they have gradually become susceptible as new races of leaf and stripe rust have evolved.

India released three multilines in 1979, and they are mixtures of 6 to 12 wheat components, each resembling 8156 but having different genes for rust resistance. The commercial availability of these mixtures will provide answers to several important questions: Will seed production be less complicated for multilines than for individual varieties? Will seed companies make smaller profits from multilines (because farmers will replace their seed less often) and therefore make less effort to sell multilines? Will seed certification agencies have difficulty determining whether a multiline conforms to a standard mixture?

Varietal mixtures

An idea tried in Western Europe is to mechanically mix two to five wheat varieties that are similar in maturity. This mixture is easily prepared with recent commercial varieties, but because the component varieties of the mixture are more diverse than the lines that make up a true multiline, there are more problems for the farmer and miller. The use of varietal mixtures requires more research to determine what characteristics varieties should have to make a suitable combination.

A comparable idea is the "spatial mixture." In Kenya a farmer may grow four to six wheat varieties in adjoining fields as a hedge against disease outbreak. If one variety becomes susceptible and an epidemic occurs, the chances are that the fields with different varieties will escape. The farmer may lose the field planted with the susceptible variety, but his harvest will not be totally destroyed as it might have been had all fields been planted to the susceptible variety.

Geographic placement of varieties

Another technique that has helped stabilize yields is strategic plantings of wheat varieties. Varieties that have demonstrated resistance to a particular disease are planted like a wall around an area where the disease pathogen is known to survive the off-season.

In northern India, for example, summer heat destroys stripe rust pathogens in the plains, but they survive in the nearby Himalayan foothills. When cool weather returns, the spores spread to newly planted wheat on the plains. To obstruct this movement, Punjab State requests farmers near the mountains to sow the resistant variety Sonalika. The barrier formed by the fields of resistant wheat check the emergence of stripe rust long enough to allow large areas planted to less-resistant varieties to escape damage during the seedling stage, thus reducing yield loss. A similar strategy is used around the Nilgiri Hills in southern India where spores of leaf and stem rust survive the summer.

Strategic placement of varieties requires good mapping of the movement of pathogens, which has been done in India by research pathologists. Strategic placement is likely to become increasingly important as a control mechanism. Governments can influence geographic placement of varieties to some degree through their seed distribution programs.

Resistance to other fungus diseases

Other than rusts, important fungus diseases include septoria, scab, helminthosporium, powdery mildew, bunt, and loose smut (see Table 10). Worldwide, the first three are the most destructive.

Septoria

Leaf blotch is caused by *Septoria tritici*. It thrives in cool regions where cloud cover, fog, and rains persist for long periods during the wheat-growing season, as in the Mediterranean basin, Argentina, and Chile. Another species, *S. nodorum*, prospers under high temperatures and causes severe losses in some years in areas like Argentina. Since septoria affects 20 percent of the wheat regions in developing countries, the stakes are high.

No high-yielding commercial wheat variety has yet been identified that has strong, stable genetic resistance to septoria—equaling, say, current resistance to stem rust. But dependable resistance is likely to be available soon. Sixty countries are growing the International Septoria Observation Nursery, Israel is screening a large collection of wheats for septoria resistance, and CIMMYT is collaborating with national programs in Brazil, Argentina, and North Africa to develop resistance under their environments.

Scab

The Chinese rate scab, which is caused by a species of *Fusarium*, as the most destructive disease of spring wheat. It lowers yields 10 percent in every year throughout the Yangtze Valley, and an epidemic breaks out every 4 to 5 years. Argentina and Brazil suffer similar losses. Since these three countries account for almost half the wheat produced by developing countries, the disease is important. Scab occurs in many areas that rotate wheat with maize, or wheat with rice.

Little research has been done on scab. Varieties with some tolerance have been identified in China, Argentina, Japan, and France, but no complete resistance has been found. CIMMYT is intercrossing the tolerant varieties and also attempting to transfer genes for scab resistance from grasses that are related to wheat. If an international campaign, comparable in scope to the work on rusts, were launched against scab, there is little doubt the disease could be substantially brought under control.

Helminthosporium

Some countries in the tropics hope to reduce their foreign exchange outlays for wheat imports by growing wheat in the cool season. At that time, however, the prevailing temperatures and humidity are still higher than those that are normal during the wheat-growing season in a temperate climate. As a result, diseases flourish. The leaf and spike (head) pathogen *Helminthosporium sativum* is particularly destructive in tropical climates. Attempts to produce wheat during the rainy season in Zambia and Tanzania have been hampered by this pathogen.

Another species, *H. gigantium*, does not affect cereals in temperate climates, but in the tropics, it moves from tropical grasses to cereals including wheat. In Central America, *H. gigantium* causes leaf and spike diseases that can kill the wheat plant. Still another species, *H. tritici repentis*, is present in many environments. At high elevations, such as in central Mexico, the Andean region, or the highlands of East Africa, this fungus is aggressive and damages much of the leaves, exposing the plants to destruction by weaker pathogens.

By evaluating thousands of wheats under tropical conditions in Mexico, CIMMYT has identified some lines that show very limited tolerance for these diseases. Crosses have been made among the lines, and the most promising progeny are being distributed to developing countries through the Tropical Helminthosporium Screening Nursery. Several million hectares might become suitable for wheat if resistance to helminthosporium species and other leaf diseases and root rots can be developed. Even so, wheat yields are not likely to be high under tropical conditions. Other food crops—such as maize, rice, and oilseeds—are better adapted to warm humid climates and will outproduce wheat in the lowland tropics whenever moisture is adequate.

Tolerance to environmental stress

Weather causes large variations in wheat yields, but there are many ways to minimize the effects of weather. The world wheat germ-plasm collection contains varieties that vary in tolerance to cold; to frost during the seedling stage; to heat and hot, dry winds; and to droughts of different lengths at varying growth stages. (The "world wheat germ-plasm collection" refers to the total wheat varieties and lines in the germ plasm banks of the world. The two largest wheat collections are held by the U.S. Department of Agriculture at Fort Collins, Colorado, and by the Vavilov Institute in Leningrad, USSR. If duplications were eliminated from all banks, the world wheat collection would consist of perhaps 30,000 entries.)

No reliable criteria for selecting wheats that can tolerate stress yet exist, but worldwide testing of the international wheat nurseries, which are grown under all types of climate, has revealed that certain wheat varieties are better adapted to extremes of weather and give higher yields than other varieties. Use of a short-season variety may be wise in areas where wheat often is hit by unseasonal frost, late drought, or hot winds at heading time. Fast-maturing varieties may escape the bad weather. Also, research on planting times may reveal changes that can be made to lower the odds that unfavorable periods of weather will strike at critical crop stages.

In wheat-growing areas near great deserts, such as in Algeria and North China, late-maturing wheats are often withered by hot winds before the grain is ripe. Yields are reduced because the grains shrivel. But breeders have been able to select varieties that have a normal growth until heading time and then ripen quickly, so the grain is usually mature by the time the hot winds begin. Such varieties yield better than short-season varieties grown under the same conditions.

In areas where the wheat crop matures during a rainy period, the kernels of some varieties are likely to germinate in the head while the plant is standing in the field, thus lowering the cereal quality. However some varieties resist sprouting, and the trait is genetically transferable.

Another environmental stress is caused by saline soil. Most saline conditions can be remedied by installing proper drainage, which is an engineering problem. But for some areas in deserts and near the sea, salt tolerance would be advantageous. Several institutions are working on this problem by seeking tolerant varieties and by making wide crosses with wheat relatives that are known to be salt tolerant.

In general, research to develop wheats that can tolerate environmental stress must be conducted in areas where the stresses occur. International research centers such as CIMMYT and ICARDA can suggest the breeding materials and research methods that are most likely to give success.

NARROWING THE YIELD GAP

Finding ways to narrow differences in yields between the experiment station and farmers' fields is another promising area for research. In India the top wheat yields on most irrigated research stations are 5000 to 5500 kg/ha, which is matched by the best farmers. But the average farmer gets only 1600 kg/ha. The yield gap is attributable to differences in seed quality, the amount of fertilizer applied, irrigation availability, thoroughness of weed control, quality of land, and the know-how of the cultivator. Every country has a yield gap that can be reduced by better agronomic practices, especially those dealing with fertilizers, weed control, and the timing of production operations.

Supplying nutrients

Any research that results in a more efficient use of fertilizer will increase yields or reduce the farmer's costs. Nitrogen is almost always deficient in wheat-growing soils, and nitrogen deficiency is to be expected in most soils where two cultivated crops are harvested each year. Phosphorus deficiency exists in many soils or may develop within a few years after high-yielding wheats, accompanied by nitrogen fertilization, are introduced. Soil potassium and micronutrients, such as sulfur and zinc, are generally adequate under traditional agriculture, but they too may be depleted by high-yielding crops. In some soil types, the farmer may need to apply chemical supplements after a decade or less. On some acid soils, application of crushed dolomitic limestone can greatly increase grain yields by reducing acidity, releasing phosphorus and adding calcium and magnesium, whose low availability otherwise limits plant growth. Fertilizer research is a continuing need for intensive agriculture.

There are ways to help the wheat farmer use fertilizer more efficiently. The basic approach is to use a modern wheat variety, which deposits a larger share of its dry matter in the grain, thus producing more kilograms of grain for each kilogram of chemical nutrients applied. Research agronomists can demonstrate this principle to the extension agents.

Three other avenues of research may raise the return on the farmer's expenditure on fertilizer: improving the efficiency of plant uptake of nutrients; fitting the fertilizer formula more precisely to soil deficiencies and plant needs; and using organic materials and legume rotations where economically feasible.

Efficiency of uptake

It has been estimated that when fertilizer is applied in temperate regions, only half the nitrogen and a third of the phosphorus and potassium applied are recovered by crops. Losses in the tropics are thought to be even greater because the air and soil temperatures tend to be higher.

The nitrogen not utilized by the plant is lost — it forms a gas that escapes into the atmosphere, or it dissolves and is carried away by soil moisture. Nitrogen losses can be reduced by incorporating the fertilizer into the soil instead of spreading it on the surface. Applying fertilizer two or three times during the crop season, rather than all at once, is another way to raise nitrogen uptake.

For phosphorus, placement is very important in achieving efficient uptake. Phosphorus is an immobile element, and it quickly reacts with the soil, which makes it unavailable to plants. Placing phosphorus fertilizer in a band near the seed, instead of broadcasting the fertilizer and tilling it into the soil, can increase efficiency of uptake, sometimes severalfold. Trials on the most economic way to place fertilizer are needed in every country.

Adjusting the fertilizer formulation

Some wheat programs recommend fertilizer rates that are excessive for one or more nutrients. For example, mixed fertilizers that are recommended to farmers often include potassium even when trials have revealed no response to that element. A nitrogen-phosphorus ratio of 2:1 is commonly recommended for irrigated wheat; and a 1:1 ratio, under rainfed conditions. But the correct ratio can best be determined by on-farm fertilizer trials.

Use of organic materials

Organic fertilizers are held by some scientists to be superior to inorganic fertilizers because organic materials contain certain micronutrients that are useful for plant growth. Organic materials also improve soil texture and water-holding capacity. But it is unrealistic to think that composts, manure, or other organic materials can significantly replace chemical fertilizers. There is not enough organic material to serve this purpose, and in most countries, the labor supply and transport system could not cope with the volume and weight that would be required to replace chemicals. Furthermore, in countries like India and Pakistan where coal and wood are scarce, nearly all cattle dung, the best organic fertilizer, is burned as cooking fuel.

The FAO analyzed compost in China and found that 1000 kilograms contained an average of 5 kilograms of nitrogen. Therefore, a Chinese village must produce and spread 4600 kilograms of compost (bulk weight) to obtain nitrogen benefits equal to those of one 50-kilogram bag of urea. Although the Chinese are leaders in the use of organic fertilizers, they also apply 10 million tons of chemical nutrients a year.

Common sense is needed. Application of organic fertilizers is a sound agricultural practice and should be used wherever the raw materials, labor supply, and transport permit. Agronomic and economic research can help farmers decide on the most efficient combination of organic and chemical fertilizers.

Weed control

Weeds cause yield loss by competing with crop plants for sunlight, moisture, and soil nutrients. With heavy weed growth, wheat yields are easily cut by half, and sometimes they are depressed to zero. Species of weeds differ greatly among countries, and control practices also vary. Research on weed control must be done location by location. Researchers in every developing country need to conduct trials both on experiment stations and on farms to find the most efficient methods of weed control.

Four common techniques are used against weeds: hand pulling, mechanical cultivation, chemical killing, and crop rotations that discourage weeds.

Hand pulling

Pulling weeds by hand is an ancient method of weed control, and it is still widely practiced in China. Weeds that are pulled are generally fed to animals. Hand weeding provides only partial control because by the time the weeders have completed one round, new weeds usually have grown large enough to compete with the wheat. Moreover the pulling process itself causes some damage to the wheat roots.

Mechanical cultivation

For many farmers, weed control takes place before the wheat is sown. They let weeds sprout, then they use a plow or mechanical cultivator to uproot the seedlings. Many agronomists argue that this is the most economical and effective type of weed control in wheat. Mechanical weed control after sowing is not possible because the wheat plants are grown too close together.

Chemical killing

Herbicides offer another approach to weed control. Some chemicals, like 2,4-D, that selectively kill broad-leaved weeds became generally available in the 1950s, and those that selectively kill grassy weeds became widely available in the 1960s and 1970s. Herbicides such as these may pose a hazard to the wheat crop and to neighboring crops if the chemicals are not applied with proper dosage, method, and timing. The hazards of herbicides have recently been reduced by recommendations that give the farmer more precise information on when and how to apply.

Use of herbicides in the Third World is expanding, and a phenomenal range of new chemicals is being created. Developing countries that choose to use herbicides must conduct their own trials, under the local environment, against the most damaging weeds.

Cropping systems that discourage weeds

Crop rotations can reduce weed populations because conditions in one crop that favor some weeds are changed when the next crop is planted. For example, a cultivated row crop followed by a solid-stand cereal crop will help suppress weeds. A 2-year wheat-fallow rotation, as is practiced on Turkey's Anatolian plateau (see Chapter 5), also controls weeds, in part through the mechanical cultivation that takes place during the fallow period. When a cereal crop and a legume crop are alternated, as in the wheat-soybean rotation of Argentina, a herbicide for broad-leaved weeds can be applied to one crop and a chemical for grassy weeds to the next, thus reducing the carry-over of weed seeds. A rotation of berseem clover or alfalfa with wheat is effective because forage crops are cut frequently. Weeds that sprout with the forage do not get an opportunity to produce seeds that would carry over to the subsequent wheat crop.

Integrated weed control

No one method will control all weeds under all conditions. Instead, farmers may need to use a combination of methods. The best mixture will depend upon local trials, local weed species, local crop rotations, and the circumstances of the farmers (that is, size of crop, labor supply, and degree of mechanization).

Insecticides and fungicides

Insects generally are of minor importance in wheat and do far less damage to wheat than they do to rice or maize, though they transmit some virus diseases of wheat. But in a few locations, under the right weather conditions, an insect may be a major pest of wheat. Examples are the sawfly and Hessian fly in parts of North Africa, the sunnipest (chinch bug) in parts of the Mideast, and the aphid in Latin America. The armyworm, the giant locust, and other general feeders, which attack almost any crop, can be destructive whenever their populations swell.

Plant breeding cannot counteract all insect problems of wheat, particularly the general feeders. A more practical remedy for the occasionally severe attacks is the use of chemical insecticides. But untimely or excessive application of insecticides can destroy the natural enemies of the insect pest, cause outbreaks of secondary pests, reduce populations of bees and other pollinators, and sometimes lead to human health problems. The country that uses insecticides will require local trials to formulate recommendations and a well-trained extension staff to advise on application.

Agricultural chemicals are like medicine. They are beneficial when used properly. But when used improperly, they may harm the crop and even prove fatal to man.

Timely production practices

The timing of land preparation, seeding, fertilizer application, weed control, and irrigation can account for much of the difference between a wheat farmer who averages 3000 kg/ha and a neighboring farmer with identical soils and climate who averages 1000 kg/ha. Every country needs agronomic trials and demonstrations that deal with timely performance of cropping activities.

Farmers' circumstances influence the timing of production practices. The farmer who cultivates by hoe, who uses oxen, or who rents machinery is less able to achieve timely operations than the farmer who has a full set of machinery under his control. Government services also affect the timing of production practices. Government services determine when credit is released to farmers, when the price of wheat is announced, when fertilizers become available, and when irrigation water reaches the fields. (These services are discussed in Chapter 7.)

ON-FARM RESEARCH

The national wheat programs that have made the greatest progress generally are the ones that conduct on-farm research and on-farm demonstrations. They test new wheat varieties outside the research station before release, and they try production practices in farmers' fields to learn how best to help the new varieties express their genetic superiority. Initial pesticide trials are best conducted on experiment stations. Other research, such as fertilizer trials, is best performed on farms because soil fertility on stations is frequently higher; hence not representative of farm conditions.

On-farm surveys greatly improve the flow of information among farmers, extension workers, and researchers. Cooperation among these groups needs to be welded. In the national wheat programs of India, Pakistan, Bangladesh, Ecuador, Chile, and Argentina, economists and biological scientists have teamed up for on-farm surveys such as:

- Studies of farmers' circumstances, which serve as the basis of planning improved technologies. "Farmers' circumstances" refers to natural conditions (climate, soils, topography of farmland, local pests, and diseases); local supplies of credit, seeds, fertilizers, and other inputs; and prices of harvested grain.

Wheat breeders attending a 6-month training course in Mexico. (*Source:* CIMMYT.)

- Studies of the consequences of new technology—for example, what happens to income distribution, to rural employment, and to national diets as a consequence of agricultural change.
- Studies of public policies and services that can hasten the adoption of modern technology.
- Studies of training procedures that will best prepare national research and extension staffs to deal with farmers' problems.

Economists and agronomists need to be trained to work together to translate their research findings into better recommendations to farmers. In using on-farm research as a tool, the economist and the agronomist should examine all the problems confronting the farmer—some of which are biological, some economic, some social, some political. Together these problems are broader than the conventional idea of agricultural research, broader even than the jurisdiction of a ministry of agriculture.

There may be no fertilizer because a country is short of foreign exchange; the credit system may be weak because national revenues are inadequate; the insufficiency of farm-to-market roads and grain storage capacity may arise from faulty investment priorities. These social, economic, and political questions must be addressed and solved somewhere in the government before the agronomic gap between the experiment station and the farmer's field can be substantially reduced.

RAISING THE YIELD POTENTIAL

The yield potential of the best spring wheats is 8500 to 9500 kg/ha, when grown by scientists in an environment of high solar radiation, with irrigation and high soil fertility, and without weeds and diseases. Yield potential is one measure of progress in wheat improvement.

The genetic yield potential of spring wheats has been increased only gradually since the early 1960s, that is, since the semi-dwarf plant type essentially doubled yield potential. This plateau does not mean that agriculture has been standing still. The average farmer's yield in the developing countries has climbed to 1400 kg/ha, an impressive rise of 64 percent since 1960, but that yield is still far below the yield potential achieved on the research station.

Future improvements in genetic yield potential may come from crossing spring-habit wheats with winter-habit wheats, from development of wheat varieties with longer or more fertile heads, and from crosses between wheat and other plant species.

Crossing spring wheats with winter wheats

Large-scale crossing of spring-habit wheats with winter-habit wheats was begun recently (the complementary strengths of the two types of wheat are discussed in Chapter 1). Before 1970, to cross the two types, pollination was generally done in laboratories and greenhouses where temperatures could be controlled to induce the winter wheats to flower at the same time as the spring wheats. A few prominent wheats were bred in this manner, such as Thatcher, a U.S. variety.

In the early 1970s, CIMMYT found a location in the Mexican

plateau where spring x winter crosses could be made in the field. There, winter wheats are seeded in November, and subsequent temperatures are low enough to vernalize the seedlings. Spring wheats are sown in the same field in January, by which time temperatures have risen enough to be safe. In May both the winter and spring wheats flower so hundreds of crosses can be made.

As a result, a large number of first-generation, or F_1, progeny are produced, and breeders can select those with desirable traits. Oregon State University (U.S.A.) receives part of the F_1 seed each year and crosses the best F_1 progeny with winter-wheat varieties or lines to transfer good spring-wheat characteristics into winter wheats. CIMMYT crosses the F_1s to the best spring wheats to improve the latter with useful characteristics of winter wheats.

The benefits of the spring x winter crossing program are beginning to show in experimental lines of spring wheats:

• In the thirteenth International Spring Bread Wheat Screening Nursery (reported in 1979), the highest-yielding lines carried winter-wheat genes.

• The single highest-yielding experimental spring wheat in 1979 was a line named Veery, which carries in its pedigree the Russian winter-wheat variety Kavkaz. The mean yield of Veery sibs (sisters) was 700 kg/ha higher than the mean of all entries in the 1979 screening nursery.

• The best resistance to *Septoria tritici* and stripe rust in the 1979 international nurseries was provided by experimental lines carrying winter genes.

• Some progeny of spring x winter crosses showed promise as facultative wheats — wheats that are intermediate between winter wheats and spring wheats — which are suitable for higher elevations in Algeria and Turkey and higher latitudes in Argentina and Chile.

Progeny from spring x winter crosses are being shared with the international nursery network. Most countries find it difficult to make spring x winter crosses since they lack a suitable climate (Iran, Turkey, Chile, and China are among the few exceptions). Spring x winter crosses may result in the first significant lifting of genetic yield potential since the advent of the semi-dwarf varieties.

Wheat plants with exceptionally long heads may be a way to achieve higher yields in the future if the tendency of these varieties to produce fewer tillers and less-plump grain can be overcome. A normal head of a high-yielding semi-dwarf is at left. (*Source:* CIMMYT.)

Longer heads, more spikelets, more fertile florets

Another prospect for raising yield potential is the creation of wheat plants with longer heads, more fertile spikelets per head, more grains per spikelet, and larger grains. Achieving any one of these characteristics would theoretically raise yield, but progress in one factor is frequently offset by losses in another.

For example, one experimental line containing the Yugoslav winter wheat Tetrastichun in its pedigree has a head twice as long as that of most spring wheats. But the yield advantage provided by longer heads has been offset by a tendency to produce fewer tillers (extra stems). This is a reflection of a normal biological correlation: As the number of grains per head increases, the number of tillers per plant decreases. Breeders are improving the trade-off between long heads and tillering ability, but problems still arise with grain plumpness (kernel weight).

In Mexico and elsewhere, breeders have developed experimental lines of wheat with eight grains per spikelet instead of the three to five that are normal in bread wheats. But in the dense plantings farmers use, maintaining this number of grains without reducing the plumpness of the grains is difficult. So far only a few lines combine more kernels with good kernel type (high 1000-kernel weight). These lines are being intercrossed.

Such research work is now concentrated among skillful breeders in the most advanced centers, and the benefits reach the developing countries through international nurseries. Prospects for raising the yield ceiling in this manner are only fair.

Durum wheat research

Although bread wheats dominate the world's wheat production, the diets of millions of people in such semi-arid areas as North Africa, the Mideast, and central India are based on durum wheat. Six objectives for durum research deserve priority.

• Durums need stronger resistance to stem and leaf rust. Durums in general are weaker than bread wheats in rust resistance, perhaps because there has been much less breeding effort on this crop than on bread wheats.

• Durums require earlier maturity in areas that are threatened by late frosts in the spring or hot winds in early summer.

• Durums require greater cold tolerance and later maturity when grown on the high plateaus of Turkey, Iraq, Iran, and Afghanistan or in southern Argentina and Chile.

• The height of durums needs to be reduced to a range of 120 to 130 centimeters in countries that have semi-arid areas and grow tall wheats (2 meters high). High-rainfall areas or areas under irrigation require short durums (75 to 100 centimeters high).

• Durums consumed as *couscous* (steamed cracked wheat) require greater vitreousness (translucent grains).

• For export, durums should have good grain quality—especially large, vitreous grains that are free of yellow berry, have highly yellow pigment, and produce strong dough (able to remain unsticky when boiled). Yellow berry, a kernel discoloration to which low-protein durum varieties are susceptible under certain weather conditions, reduces the commercial value of the grain.

For durum breeding, a crossing block with a broad range of plant characteristics is required.

Triticale: A wide cross

The man-made cereal triticale is a cross between wheat and rye. Modern work on triticale began in Canada at the University of Manitoba in the 1950s and was greatly expanded during the next decade by a joint program between Manitoba and CIMMYT. Since then triticale has made spectacular progress. Average triticale yields in international trials rose from less than a third of the yields of bread wheat to approximate parity (7800 kg/ha). Triticale now is superior to wheat in resistance to stem and stripe rust, *Septoria tritici*, powdery mildew, and smuts. But triticale generally does not yet have the plump grains of the best bread wheats. This is an important limitation in marketing and is the major focus of continuing research.

A number of wheat programs in developing countries share in this triticale research — notably Argentina, Brazil, Chile, India, Kenya, and Tanzania. Argentina is studying dual-purpose triticale, which can be grazed by sheep and then allowed to resume growth so it can be later harvested as a grain crop. In Kenya triticale planted in the traditional wheat zone — a high, cool environment — outproduces bread wheat by 30 to 60 percent because of its disease resistance and tolerance to acid soils.

Triticale was tested at more than 90 sites worldwide in the 1970s, and it deserves even more research emphasis, especially in those environments in which triticale has outperformed wheat — in acid soils (Brazil) and in cool highland areas (Himalayan, East African, and Andean).

Other wide crosses

Although triticale has the most research behind it, other wide crosses are under study. The objective in most of these crosses is not to develop new cereals but to transfer genes for greater disease resistance, tolerance to environmental stress, or better nutritional value to wheat. CIMMYT has made crosses between bread wheat and barley, and between wheat and its near relatives—*Hordeum, Agropyron,* and *Elymus.* These crosses suffer various genetic malfunctions so the progeny are only partially fertile. But for the most part, derived plants can be crossed back to wheat to obtain some seed set.

China has made rapid advances in this field. It has released a number of small grain varieties based upon wide crosses. Most developing countries, however, will find wide-cross work does not fit their research priorities. Industrialized countries are more likely to be able to afford the risk capital, and the benefits, when demonstrated, will appear in the international nursery trials.

10
Prospects for Wheat
in the 1980s and 1990s

Administrators involved with wheat need to concern themselves not only with technology, but also with certain broad issues, which, if not dealt with wisely, could frustrate efforts to provide enough food during the rest of this century. Those issues are population growth, population pressure on land, fertilizer production prospects, the outlook for the international wheat trade, and the place of wheat in the diets of developing countries.

World population growth

Rising population sets the marching orders for people concerned with food production. About 12,000 years ago, humans learned to grow crops and to domesticate animals, thus providing a more secure source of food. These agricultural beginnings occurred when the world contained about 15 million people. Under the new way of life, the population began to multiply more rapidly, and by A.D. 1, the world's population had doubled four times in 10,000 years, to 250 million. Another doubling was completed in 1650 years, bringing the population to 500 million. The next doubling, to 1000 million, required only 200 years. About that time (1850), the death rate began to decline as a result of improved sanitation, the discovery of the causes of infectious diseases, and the dawn of modern medicine. Another doubling of the population, to 2000 million, occurred by 1930 — in only 80 years. Then sulfa drugs, antibiotics, and improved vaccines reduced death rates still further. By 1975 world population had doubled once more, to 4000 million; that doubling took only 45 years.

If population growth continues at the same rate, the next doubling will be completed by 2015, and food production would need

Table 11
Population projections in selected wheat-growing countries

Country	Population (millions)			Population increase to end of century (%)
	Estimate mid-1980	Projected mid-2000	Projected ultimate	
Algeria	19.0	36.9	93.6	94
Egypt	42.1	64.9	90.0	54
Ethiopia	32.6	55.3	136.5	70
Kenya	15.9	32.3	93.8	103
Libya	3.0	5.7	11.7	90
Morocco	21.0	37.3	70.9	78
Sudan	18.7	31.8	88.8	70
Tunisia	6.5	9.7	14.4	49
Afghanistan	15.9	26.4	65.8	66
Bangladesh	90.6	156.7	334.5	73
China, PR[a]	975.0	1,212.3	1,530.0	24
India	676.2	976.2	1,642.8	44
Iran	38.5	66.1	101.0	72
Iraq	13.2	24.5	49.1	86
Jordan	3.2	5.9	11.8	84
Korea, DPR	17.9	27.4	42.9	53
Mongolia	1.7	2.7	3.9	59
Nepal	14.0	22.0	51.4	57
Pakistan	86.5	152.0	334.6	76
Syria	8.6	16.2	32.7	88
Turkey	45.5	69.6	97.8	53
Argentina	27.1	32.9	41.0	21
Brazil	122.0	205.1	341.0	68
Chile	11.3	15.2	18.6	35
Mexico	68.2	128.9	203.5	89
Peru	17.6	29.2	54.6	66
Uruguay	2.9	3.5	4.5	21
All developing countries	3,283	4,884	6,260	49
Australia	14.6	17.9	18.5	23
Canada	24.0	29.0	30.3	21
France	53.6	57.5	60.7	7
U.K.	55.8	56.5	60.1	1
U.S.	222.5	260.4	265.5	17
USSR	266.0	311.0	360.0	17
All developed countries	1,131	1,272	2,040	12

[a]Projection for China was made before the government announced its policy to limit families to one child by 1985.

Source: Population Reference Bureau, World population data sheet.

to double in the same 40-year period or sooner. Fortunately there is some evidence that population growth has begun to slow. Yet even if the next doubling takes 60, or 80, years, the necessary increase of food production is staggering. In essence, within 40 to 80 years, world food production must be increased by as much again as the increase in the last 12,000 years — since the beginning of agriculture.

National wheat programs are being subjected to great pressures by population growth. The prospective population increases by the end of the century suggest food production targets that few developing countries are likely to attain (see Table 11), and the population that will be reached before birth and death rates balance would call for food increases in some countries that are clearly impossible for the agriculture of today.

The data in Table 11 have varying degrees of reliability. The populations estimated for mid-1980 are the most firm. The projection of the population to the end of the century, based on trends before 1980, would prove wrong if a country were to experience a change of growth rate that was not visible in recent trends. The projected ultimate population that each country may have when it attains zero population growth is highly speculative. For all developing countries, this projection carries into the twenty-first century, and for a few, into the twenty-second century.

Regardless of whether the projections are precise, they demonstrate the disaster toward which the world is headed if the population growth trends of the 1970s are permitted to run their full course. Every agricultural administrator will find it advantageous to know the projected population growth for his country and to participate in national policy discussions on the prospects for having adequate food supplies.

Land pressure

Another ominous measure of population growth is the number of people who depend on each arable hectare. In 1980 the developing countries had about 750 million hectares of arable land (land producing either annual or perennial crops), which supported 3283 million people. In other words, there were about 4 persons dependent upon each hectare.

In the year 2000, 4884 million people will be dependent upon the same 750 million hectares, that is more than six persons will be seeking food from each hectare. This calculation assumes that the amount of arable land will not increase. Although some land now in forests or pasture will be plowed up for crops by the year 2000, and multiple cropping (growing more than one crop on the same land within 12 months) will increase, there will also be shrinkage of cropland in most countries through the encroachment of cities and diversion to other nonagricultural uses. The result will be an approximate stability in crop area.

The population pressure in individual developing countries varies widely (see Table 12). Argentina has only 1 person per hectare of arable land, but Egypt has 15 persons per hectare. By the turn of the century, it is projected that Egypt will have 23 persons per hectare. When pressure reaches that level, it must be assumed that a substantial part of the population will be earning its income from nonagricultural activities and that much of the nation's food supply will be imported.

The problem is how to create nonagricultural employment that does not further congest the primary cities. China and South Korea have achieved considerable success in village-level industries, and Mexico seeks to decentralize its major industries to secondary towns. However, imaginative new solutions are still needed.

Fertilizer production outlook

Future supplies of fertilizers, especially nitrogen, are another cause for anxiety. Chemical fertilizers have been the driving force behind rising crop yields, and one economist has calculated that 54 percent of the grain yield increase since World War II can be attributed to a greater use of fertilizer. World consumption of chemical fertilizers has risen from fewer than 1 million tons of nutrients in 1906 to more than 100 million tons in 1980. Since 1945 fertilizer use has nearly doubled every 10 years.

If production of wheat and other cereals has to increase by 50 percent by the end of the century, the demand for chemical fertilizer has to increase at least proportionately. New chemical factories will require immense investments. One fertilizer planner has calculated that each population increase of 6 million people requires 1 additional thousand-ton-a-day ammonia plant and 3 urea

Table 12
Population pressure in selected wheat-growing countries, 1980 and 2000

Country	Arable hectares (millions)	Persons per arable hectare	
		1980	2000
Algeria	7.5	2.5	5.0
Egypt	2.8	15.0	23.0
Morocco	7.9	3.0	5.0
Tunisia	4.4	1.5	2.0
Bangladesh	9.1	10.0	15.0
China, PR	99.6	10.0	12.0
India	168.5	4.0	6.0
Pakistan	20.0	4.0	7.0
Turkey	28.0	1.6	2.5
Argentina	35.1	1.0	1.0
Brazil	40.7	3.0	5.0
Chile	5.8	2.0	2.6
Mexico	23.2	3.0	6.0
All developing countries	741.0	4.4	6.6
Australia	42.7	0.3	0.4
Canada	44.3	0.5	0.7
France	18.9	2.8	3.0
U.K.	7.0	8.0	8.1
U.S.	191.5	1.2	1.4
USSR	231.8	1.2	1.3
All developed countries	672.0	1.7	1.9

Sources: FAO *Production yearbook;* Population Reference Bureau, *World population data sheet.*

units (to convert the ammonia to solid fertilizer). So with the world's population increasing by 70 million to 75 million people a year, 12 new ammonia factories and 36 new urea factories are needed annually, at a cost of $3100 million a year. Scientists have so far found no easy substitutes such as switching to organic manures or increasing the fixation of biological nitrogen.

Despite the high cost of nitrogen factories, the chief problem is not the investment but the uncertain availability of feedstocks—the raw materials for manufacturing nitrogen fertilizer. At present about 95 percent of nitrogen fertilizer is produced from synthetic ammonia, which is derived from natural gas or crude oil. Ammonia can also be made from coal as is done in hundreds of small factories in China.

The outlook for feedstocks has been assessed by the International Fertilizer Development Center, and it estimated that the known world reserves of petroleum, natural gas, and coal would last 30, 46, and 1600 years, respectively, at 1977 rates of use. Those estimates give reasonable assurance that nitrogen fertilizer produced from petroleum and natural gas will be available until the turn of the century, but not much beyond.

As reserves of natural gas and crude oil dwindle, nitrogen fertilizer will be produced by older and costlier processes in which coal or electrolysis of water provides the hydrogen needed to form synthetic ammonia. Hence nitrogen fertilizers will still be available, but at higher prices, and the cost of food will increase. It is not unrealistic to foresee a time when legislators will debate the priority uses of the remaining fossil fuels, whether for consumption in fertilizer factories to serve the food supply or for the pleasure of driving family automobiles.

Outlook for wheat in international trade

The majority of the developing countries experienced shortages of cereal grains during the 1970s. The shortages are shown by imports of wheat (see Table 13), which exceeded imports of all other cereals combined. During the 1970s, annual wheat exports rose from 53 million tons to 80 million tons. That enormous quantity of food depended largely on the agricultural performance of five exporting countries—the United States, Canada, Australia, France, and Argentina.

Developing countries increased their wheat imports by over 50 percent to almost 46 million tons during the 1970s. This expansion exceeded the rate of population growth in those countries. The rising per capita consumption of wheat was stimulated in part by the shift of population from farms to cities and in part by price, since wheat costs about half as much as rice.

Developing countries now consume about 150 million tons of wheat annually, of which a third comes from abroad. Fourteen of

Table 13
Major wheat-trading countries

Country	Net trade (million tons)			
	1968–1970 avg.	1971–1973 avg.	1974–1976 avg.	1977–1979 avg.
Exports				
United States	14.2	26.2	30.6	31.8
Canada	9.6	13.7	11.2	14.4
Australia	6.5	8.0	7.1	8.7
France	5.5	6.6	8.5	8.2
Argentina	2.4	2.0	2.3	4.1
All exporters	53.0	68.3	70.1	80.4
Imports				
Algeria	0.5	1.1	1.9	2.0
Egypt	1.7	2.0	3.3	4.8
Morocco	0.4	0.6	1.3	1.5
Nigeria	0.2	0	0.5	1.0
Bangladesh	0.4	1.4	1.7	1.0
China, PR	4.7	5.0	4.2	8.3
India	3.8	1.5	6.0	0.5
Iran	0.2	0.9	1.1	1.1
Iraq	0.1	0.6	0.6	1.2
Korea, Rep.	0.5	1.9	1.5	1.9
Pakistan	0.7	0.9	0.5	1.3
Vietnam	0.5	1.2	0.5	1.3
Brazil	2.3	2.2	2.8	3.5
Cuba	1.0	0.9	1.0	1.1
Mexico	0	0.5	0.6	0.7
All importing developing countries	26.8	32.1	40.8	45.8
Belgium	0.9	1.1	0.5	0.3
Czechoslovakia	1.2	1.1	0.6	0.6
Germany, DR	1.4	1.7	1.2	0.8
Germany, FR	1.9	2.2	1.0	–
Italy	1.2	1.5	2.2	2.3
Japan	4.1	4.7	5.6	5.7
Netherlands	1.3	1.4	0.8	0.5
Poland	1.0	1.5	1.8	2.6
United Kingdom	4.3	3.9	3.3	3.0
USSR	1.5	4.2	6.7	9.0
All importing developed countries	23.4	33.0	30.1	36.9

Source: FAO *Trade yearbook.*

the 15 developing countries that are the largest wheat importers imported more wheat at the end of the 1970s than at the beginning of the decade (see Table 13). Together these 15 countries accounted for two thirds of the developing world's wheat imports.

In the future, however, international trade is not likely to be the major source of the increased amounts of wheat that will be consumed by developing countries. With the exception of Argentina, the large exporting countries probably cannot expand their wheat production by 50 percent, which would be necessary if the rising populations of developing countries were to be fed primarily by wheat imports. Moreover, developing countries lack the foreign exchange to purchase 50 percent more wheat, and even if they had the foreign exchange, such a monumental movement of grain would overwhelm their ports and probably the world's merchant fleet as well. In addition, rapidly rising freight charges for shipping grain are restraining trade expansion. Rates increased threefold during the 1970s. The cost of shipping wheat from U.S. Gulf ports to Rotterdam (the transshipping point for much grain enroute to Asia and Africa) rose from $6.28 to $17.25 a ton; the cost from U.S. Gulf ports to India rose from $15.87 to $52.13 a ton. In the future, inflation is likely to push the costs of both grain and transportation still higher.

Can wheat maintain its share in the developing world's diet?

It is hazardous to make projections about the future food supply. In the mid-1960s, forecasters predicted a food catastrophe because a 2-year drought had struck India and Pakistan. Less than 5 years later, the green revolution had its first results, and its potentials were overestimated, suggesting that all food problems were solved. Within another 5 years, the poor harvests of 1972–1975 produced new predictions of doom, but by the end of the 1970s, world food stocks had again been rebuilt, and there was widespread complacency. That condition cannot last long, because the fickleness of weather guarantees at least one food crisis of global proportions in the 1980s and at least one in the 1990s. In fact a precarious balance between food and people is the best that can be expected until a demographic equilibrium is achieved, and even then the uncertainties of weather will remain.

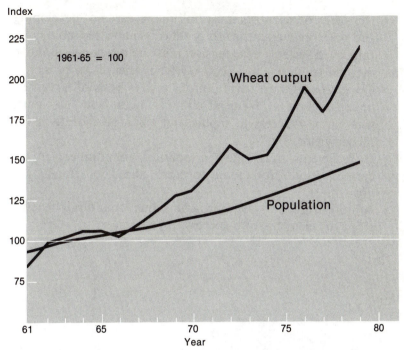

Figure 10. Changes in population and wheat production in developing countries, 1961–1979. (*Source:* FAO *Production yearbook, 1978.*)

Projections about food are based largely on past performances and especially on recent trends. In the 1970s, wheat production in the developing countries rose substantially faster than population growth (see Figure 10). We believe that new agricultural technology can enable most developing countries to meet their food needs until the end of the century largely from domestic production, even if population rises 50 percent. We believe the world has only begun to exploit the potential for higher agricultural productivity. Agricultural research is the catalyst that can trigger national efforts to expand the food supply. The odds are against dramatic breakthroughs of the type scored by semi-dwarf wheats, however. Steady increments rather than quantum jumps are to be expected.

We remind ourselves that scientists do not produce crops, farmers do. Success in growing more food requires a number of indirect and costly steps by governments.

- Networks of scientists must link the research of developing and developed countries to produce suitable technology.
- Improved systems of extension must be developed to move the new technologies effectively from scientist to farmer.
- Governments must form policies on the basis of a realistic understanding of farmers' circumstances, and they must give farmers access to inputs and financial incentives for higher yields.
- Governments must show a political commitment to increased food production to keep ahead of population growth.
- Administrators of wheat programs must obtain full benefits from the elements of a successful program.

Appendix:
Where to Get Wheat Assistance

Most developing countries have received technical assistance for their wheat programs. National programs described in this book have all participated in the international exchange of wheat technology.

A comprehensive directory of organizations that provide financial and, in some cases technical, assistance for agriculture is *Agricultural assistance sources*, published by the International Agricultural Development Service. For each organization, the directory describes the kinds of assistance offered, geographic interests, and the names of the principal officers concerned with agriculture. This directory is a good starting place for a government seeking assistance. It is available from IADS, 1611 North Kent Street, Arlington, Virginia 22209, U.S.A.

INTERNATIONAL
AGRICULTURAL RESEARCH CENTERS

A worldwide network of thirteen agricultural research centers and services are sponsored by a wide range of countries and organizations that make up the Consultative Group on International Agricultural Research. Two of the centers have programs involving wheat.

International Maize and
Wheat Improvement Center (CIMMYT)
Apdo. Postal 6-641, Mexico 6 D.F. Mexico

Within the network of research centers, the most extensive technical assistance program for wheat is provided by Centro Internacional de Mejoramiento de Maiz y Trigo (International Maize and Wheat Improvement Center). Headquartered at El Batan, 50 kilometers northeast of

Mexico City, CIMMYT uses three major research stations and many smaller testing sites in Mexico, which, in combination, are representative of the environments of spring-wheat regions in most developing countries. Hence the results obtained from CIMMYT research have been found to be widely applicable in developing countries.

CIMMYT's activities are built around its research and training in Mexico, its worldwide testing program in many environments, and its consulting work with governments. Research embraces plant breeding, agronomy studies, physiology, pathology, cereal quality, and economics. The research is conducted by a staff of two dozen senior scientists, postdoctoral fellows, and visiting scientists of 15 to 20 nationalities. In addition eight to ten senior scientists are posted in regional or national programs of developing countries. In 1981 outposted staff were assigned to the Andean and Southern Cone regions of South America, North and West Africa, the East African highlands, the Mideast, South Asia, and Pakistan's national wheat program.

Each year the CIMMYT wheat staff distributes about 40 nurseries to participating scientists. Each nursery contains seed of 20 to 500 wheat varieties or lines. Trials are planted by participants at 2300 sites in 115 countries. Some trials seek limited information about the adaptation of wheat to particular environments or resistance to specific diseases. Other nurseries provide comparisons of wheat yields on a worldwide basis, thus measuring wide adaptation. Data from the trials are assembled and published by CIMMYT and returned to the participants. National scientists may enter their own promising materials in the nurseries to test for wide adaptation, tolerance to stresses, and disease resistance.

CIMMYT scientists visit most of the 115 countries annually. These experienced senior scientists observe the results of trials, advise on local wheat research programs, discuss production problems in farmers' fields, and help select the 40 to 60 young scientists who are invited to Mexico each year for one cropping season of experience in wheat research or production.

As time permits, CIMMYT's training staff is lent to national programs to help organize local training courses of a few weeks' duration, especially for extension workers, whose numbers are so large that they cannot all be sent to a foreign training course.

CIMMYT's publications office issues two annual reports dealing with wheat: *CIMMYT review*, in layman's language for nonscientists, and *Wheat improvement*, which contains research results for the hundreds of participants in the wheat network. In addition the periodical *CIMMYT today* provides comprehensive essays on such topics as winter x spring crosses, off-season nurseries, or progress in triticale breeding. From time

to time, CIMMYT publishes manuals for researchers in developing countries. Examples are a guide for the identification of wheat diseases and a
manual on farm surveys.

International Center for Agricultural Research in Dry Areas (ICARDA)
P.O. Box 5466 Aleppo, Syria

ICARDA, with its principal research station located near Aleppo, has
both regional and worldwide responsibilities. The region it serves is the
Near East and North Africa, where it works to improve rainfed
agriculture and the well-being of the rural community. ICARDA serves
as a worldwide center for the improvement of barley, faba beans, and
lentils. ICARDA focuses its regional work on bread wheat, durum
wheat, triticale, chickpeas, and forage crops. The crops are studied in a
farming-systems context.

The cereal improvement program—one of four research programs at
ICARDA—has a staff of nine scientists supported by research associates
and assistants who use ICARDA's main research station as the base for a
breeding program for bread wheat, durum wheat, barley, and triticale.
The four crops are studied also in agronomy, pathology, grain quality,
and entomology research projects. Cereal trials are conducted on substa-
tions elsewhere in Syria and in farmers' fields in various agroclimatic
zones.

Bread wheat improvement at ICARDA is conducted in collaboration
with CIMMYT, and there are close links with other national and international research institutions. The cereal program also has collaborative
projects with some countries of the region, notably Jordan, Tunisia, and
Cyprus. The ICARDA farming systems program is studying the soil-
water and nutrient relations of cereal crops as well as crop rotations and
economic aspects.

The cereal program distributes nurseries to cooperators in Asia and
Africa and to locations elsewhere on request. The nurseries include
observation nurseries, regional yield trials, disease-screening nurseries,
segregating populations, and genetic stocks for crossing programs.
ICARDA has a large collection of cereal germ plasm, which is actively
evaluated. The collection includes more than 15,000 lines of barley and a
similar number of durum wheats.

Training forms an important part of ICARDA's work. Each year 15 to
20 junior-level research scientists spend 6 months working with ICARDA
in Aleppo. Trainees spend approximately 70 percent of their time in the
field and 30 percent in the classroom. Trainees are introduced to the

farming-systems research approach followed by ICARDA, and visits are made to villages where ICARDA's surveys and studies are conducted.

ICARDA researchers travel widely in the region, and visits to ICARDA, which last up to several months, are arranged for cooperating researchers. ICARDA's work is supported by publications including an annual report, newsletters, scientific discussion papers, and conference proceedings.

DISTRIBUTORS OF INTERNATIONAL WHEAT NURSERIES

Aside from international nurseries distributed by CIMMYT and ICARDA, there are three important sources of wheat nurseries. The U.S. Department of Agriculture distributes the International Spring Wheat Rust Nursery (USDA, Agricultural Research Center, Beltsville, Maryland 20705, U.S.A.). The University of Nebraska distributes the International Winter Wheat Performance Nursery (Experiment Station, Institute of Agriculture and Natural Resources, University of Nebraska, Lincoln, Nebraska 68583, U.S.A.), and Oregon State University distributes the Winter x Spring Wheat Screening Nursery (Oregon State University, Crop Science Department, Corvallis, Oregon 97331, U.S.A.).

AGRICULTURAL BUSINESSES

International corporations that sell agricultural materials such as seeds, fertilizers, pesticides, and machinery often give modest financial grants for agricultural research involving their own products. They also conduct useful field demonstrations, training courses in the use of their products, and technical guidance on agricultural research.

Glossary

Agronomy. The practice of producing agricultural crops. The art and science of crop production.

Amino acids. The building blocks that make up proteins; organic compounds that contain nitrogen. *See also* Essential amino acids.

Bran. The coarse outer covering of the wheat kernel, which is removed during milling. Whole-wheat flour contains considerable bran and, hence, is higher in protein, in nutritive value, and in fiber than white flour milled from the same grain.

Cereal. Any grass species that is grown for its edible seeds.

Continental climate. Climate characterized by extreme temperature difference between summer and winter.

Crop rotation. A repeated sequence of crops grown in the same field over a period of more than 1 year, generally designed to produce increased harvest per year; to safeguard soil; to build fertility; and to prevent the buildup of insects, diseases, and weeds.

Cultural practices. All operations involved in growing a crop such as tilling, planting, fertilizing, irrigating, and pest management.

Denitrification. The loss of nitrogen from the soil by conversion of nitrogen-containing compounds to gaseous forms of nitrogen, which then escape into the atmosphere.

Dormancy. A resting and maturing period for seed after harvest; required by some seed before germination can be initiated. Also, dormancy refers to the cessation of vegetative growth in a plant (e.g., in winter-habit wheat, conditioned by the onset of low temperature).

Durum wheat. A type of wheat with very hard grain, often used to make pasta products such as macaroni, spaghetti, and noodles. Durum wheat contains 14 chromosome pairs in contrast with the 21 pairs found in bread wheats.

Dwarf. See Semi-dwarf and dwarf.

Endosperm. The starchy inner portion of a kernel, which remains after the hull, bran, and germ have been removed by milling.

Essential amino acids. Amino acids that the human body cannot synthesize and which therefore must be obtained through diet.

Facultative wheat. Wheat that does not require a cold period before it will flower, that has a moderate level of winterhardiness, and that consequently can be planted in certain locations in autumn or spring.

Fallow. A period when the soil is kept free of plants so that moisture can be stored and nutrient levels can be built up.

Floret. The individual flower of grasses, including cereals like wheat.

Gene. The basic unit of inheritance. The carrier of genetic material from parent to offspring.

Gene bank. A storage facility for seeds of numerous varieties. To maintain viability, the seeds are generally kept at low temperature and low humidity.

Genus. The main subdivision of a family of plants or animals, made up of a group of species or of one species. A class of plants or animals with many common distinguishing characteristics. For example, genus *Triticum* is a subunit of the family *Gramineae* (grasses), and *Triticum* is further subdivided into species such as *Triticum aestivum* (bread wheat) or *Triticum durum* (durum wheat).

Germ plasm. Term used by plant breeders to refer to plants and their heritable characteristics.

Gluten. An elastic protein substance in wheat flour, which gives cohesiveness and elasticity to dough. When leavened dough ferments, the gluten traps minute bubbles of carbon dioxide, which cause the dough to rise.

Harvest index. The ratio of grain weight to total aboveground dry weight of the plant. For example, if the weight of the grain is half the total weight of the plant, the harvest index is said to be 0.5 or 50 percent.

Head. See Spike.

Heading date. Calendar date when a given proportion (usually half) of the heads in a plot have emerged. A measure of the length of the vegetative growing period.

Land race. A primitive plant variety of unknown pedigree. Sometimes called "farmer's variety" because the origin is unknown.

Lodging. Falling over of plants, which tends to affect grain filling adversely. Most common when plants that are tall and have weak stems are grown under moderate or high fertility, or when high winds or heavy rains strike the crop after heading.

Mediterranean climate. A climate in which summers are dry and hot and rainfall is concentrated in winter. Temperatures during winter are mild.

Millfeed. Any by-product of the milling industry used for feeding livestock.

Multiple cropping. Growing more than one crop on the same land within 12 months. Agronomists distinguish many forms of multiple cropping; e.g., sequential cropping (one crop following another), intercropping (two or more crops grown simultaneously in alternating rows on the same land), relay cropping (one crop planted between the rows of a maturing crop to save time in the crop rotation), and mixed cropping (two or more crops grown together with no row arrangement).

Nitrification. The biological transformation of ammonium nitrogen in the soil to oxidized forms of nitrogen (nitrite, nitrate). The modified forms of nitrogen are often leached from the soil if excess water from irrigation or rain drains through the soil.

Pasta. A general term for such wheat products as macaroni, spaghetti, and noodles, which are often made from durum wheat flour.

Pathogen. A parasite that causes disease.

Pedigree. An outline of the ancestry of a plant. A method of plant breeding that records the descent from generation to generation.

Pollination. The transfer of pollen from the male reproductive organ (anther) to the female organ (stigma).

Population. In plant breeding, a group of plants of the same species that have similar characteristics and are kept in a group to achieve breeding objectives.

Progenitor. In plant breeding, a plant used as a parent in a crossing program.

Progeny. In plant breeding, all plants tracing back to a common cross.

Rogue. An off-type plant in a plot; also, to remove off-type plants from a plot.

Semi-dwarf and dwarf. Nonscientific terms used for varieties of wheat that are short. In Mexico the term *dwarf* is applied to wheat with a height of less than 90 centimeters (sometimes 50 centimeters or less); and the term *semi-dwarf*, to those with heights of 90 to 110 centimeters. The terms one-gene and two-gene dwarf are sometimes used for wheat varieties that carry one or two dwarfing genes from the Japanese wheat variety Norin 10. In this book, the term *semi-dwarf* is used descriptively for all short wheats.

Species. A distinct kind of animal or plant, such as wheat. The subdivision of a genus. *See* Genus.

Spike. The head, or ear, of the wheat plant; carries the spikelets, which develop flowers and after pollination give rise to kernels.

Spikelet. One unit of wheat flowers. Each spikelet commonly produces three to five kernels.

Spring wheat. A wheat that grows continuously from sowing until maturity. In areas where winters are severe, spring wheats may be planted in the spring to ripen in summer, but in areas where there is little or no winter freezing, spring wheats may be planted in the autumn to ripen in the spring.

Test weight. The weight of grain measured by some common measure of volume. This is a test of the size and density of the grain.

Tiller. An extra stem that grows from the base of the plant. Varieties that have the genetic capacity to put out many extra stems are called "high-tillering varieties."

Trap nursery. A research plot in which short rows of many commercial varieties of wheat are planted in order to observe which pathogens attack them.

Variety. A wheat that is genetically uniform. In many countries, varieties are approved, named, and released by the government.

Vector. An insect or other organism that transmits a pathogen. For example, the English grain aphid sometimes transmits the barley yellow dwarf virus.

Vernalization. Induction of flowering in winter-habit wheats by exposure to a period of cold temperature. Winter-habit wheats do not flower without vernalization.

Wide adaptation. Ability of a plant to grow well in many environments.

Wide cross. A cross between two plants that do not normally hybridize, such as between two genera (wheat x barley).

Winter wheat. A wheat that requires vernalization (exposure to a cold period) before it can begin flowering. Winter wheat is sown, and generally germinates, in autumn. It is dormant in winter, resumes growth in the early spring, forms heads as day-length requirements are satisfied, and matures in summer. Winter wheats have varying levels of winterhardiness. In areas where winter wheats can survive, they generally utilize the moisture more efficiently than spring wheats and mature before the onset of summer heat; consequently their yield is greater.

Annotated Bibliography

Listed below are the publications that provided much of the information for this book. Entries are grouped by chapters. Out-of-print publications have been omitted.

Chapter 1. The Importance of Wheat and Its Principal Characteristics

Aykroyd, W. R., and Doughty, Joyce. 1971. *Wheat in human nutrition.* Rome: FAO. 163 pp.
 Discusses the basic characteristics of wheat, its production, forms in which it is eaten, and its role in world nutrition; contains a good bibliography.

Evans, L. T., ed. 1975. *Crop physiology.* Cambridge: Cambridge University Press. 374 pp.
 Twenty authorities analyze the basis of higher yields in nine crops, including wheat.

FAO. 1980. *1979 production yearbook.* Vol. 33. Rome. 309 pp.
 Contains data on area, yield, and production for about 100 crops and information on land use and population in most countries of the world. One of an annual series.

Quisenberry, K. S., and Reitz, L. P. 1967. *Wheat and wheat improvement.* Madison, Wis.: American Society of Agronomy. 560 pp.
 A widely used book. Its treatment of wheat diseases is outstanding, and the chapters on marketing, storage, and transport of wheat are authoritative.

Chapter 2. The Modern Wheat Plant and the New Technology

Dalrymple, Dana G. 1978. *Development and spread of high-yielding varieties of wheat and rice in the less developed countries.* Foreign

Agricultural Economic Report, no. 95. Washington, D.C.: U.S. Department of Agriculture. 134 pp.
> Contains data on the spread of high-yielding wheats through 1976–1977; discusses the history of Japanese dwarf and Mexican semi-dwarf wheats.

_____ . 1980. *Development and spread of semi-dwarf varieties of wheat and rice in the United States.* Agricultural Economic Report, no. 455. Washington, D.C.: U.S. Department of Agriculture. 150 pp.
> Traces the introduction and breeding of semi-dwarf wheats in the United States.

Scobie, Grant M. 1979. *Investment in international agricultural research: some economic dimensions.* World Bank Staff Working Paper, no. 361. Washington, D.C.: World Bank. 98 pp.
> The best survey of the economic and social consequences of the green revolution; based on a review of 529 books and articles.

Chapter 3. Mexico: A Pioneer

Borlaug, Norman E. 1968. Wheat breeding and its impact on world food supply. In *Proceedings, Third International Wheat Genetics Symposium*, ed. K. W. Finlay and K. W. Shepherd, pp. 1–36. Canberra: Australian Academy of Science.
> Describes the wheat revolution in Mexico, Pakistan, and India up to 1968.

_____ . 1981. Increasing and stabilizing food production. In *Plant breeding II*, ed. Kenneth J. Fry, pp. 467–492. Ames: Iowa State University Press.
> Describes, among other world food problems, leaf rust epidemics in Mexico in 1977 and Pakistan in 1978.

International Maize and Wheat Improvement Center. 1979. *CIMMYT report on wheat improvement 1979.* Mexico City. 320 pp.
> Gives technical results of CIMMYT's wheat research in Mexico. The series is published annually.

_____ . 1980. *CIMMYT review, 1980.* Mexico City. 110 pp.
> Summarizes CIMMYT's activities for wheat improvement in the preceding calendar year. An annual series.

Rockefeller Foundation. 1981. *Agricultural sciences seminar*. Working Papers. New York. 263 pp.
Discusses past and future agricultural activities of the foundation.

Skovmand, B., and Rajaram, S. 1978. *Semi-dwarf bread wheats: Names, parentage, pedigrees, origin*. Mexico City: International Maize and Wheat Improvement Center. 16 pp.
Lists wheat varieties bred and released in Mexico, their pedigrees, and names given to these varieties when released outside Mexico.

Stakman, E. C.; Bradfield, Richard; and Mangelsdorf, Paul C. 1967. *Campaigns against hunger*. Cambridge, Mass.: Harvard University Press. 328 pp.
Traces the history of Rockefeller Foundation assistance to agriculture in developing countries, 1940–1966, including the wheat programs of Mexico and India.

U.S., Department of Agriculture, Economic Research Service. 1970. *Economic progress of agriculture in developing countries, 1950–68*. Foreign Agricultural Economic Report, no. 59. Washington, D.C. 179 pp.
Case studies on agricultural growth in seven countries including Mexico, India, and Brazil.

Chapter 4. India and Pakistan: The Asian Leaders

Esso Pakistan Fertilizer Company. 1976. *Proceedings of wheat production seminar 1976*. Lahore. 255 pp.
Contains 34 papers on breeding, agronomy, pests, and farmers' constraints in Pakistan.

Gill, Khem Singh. 1979. Research on wheat and triticale in the Punjab. Mimeographed. Ludhiana: Punjab Agricultural University. 131 pp.
A comprehensive review of wheat improvement in one of India's leading agricultural states.

Indian Agricultural Research Institute. 1978. Annual reports on the All-India Coordinated Wheat Improvement Project, 1977–78. Mimeographed. New Delhi: Indian Council of Agricultural Research.
Four reports dealing with wheat and triticale trials, wheat physiology, wheat agronomy, and wheat pathology.

Indian Council of Agricultural Research. 1975. *Agronomy of dwarf wheats.* New Delhi. 94 pp.
  Summarizes the agronomic research conducted in India, 1964–1973, which was the basis for recommendations to Indian farmers.

_____ . 1978. *Wheat research in India.* New Delhi. 244 pp.
  Contains 15 well-documented papers on wheat in India.

Muhammed, Amir. 1978. *Wheat production in Pakistan.* Islamabad: Pakistan Agricultural Research Council. 19 pp.
  Gives figures on wheat production in Pakistan and discusses future problems.

Streeter, Carroll P. 1969. *A partnership to improve food production in India.* New York: Rockefeller Foundation. 137 pp.
  Describes the collaboration between the Rockefeller Foundation and India on agricultural research, including wheat research.

Vyas, V. S. 1975. *India's high-yielding varieties program in wheat, 1966-72.* Mexico City: International Maize and Wheat Improvement Center. 36 pp.
  An "adoption study" commissioned by the CIMMYT economics program to analyze why some farmers adopt new technology and others do not.

Chapter 5. Turkey: A Dryland Success

Breth, Steven A. 1977. *Turkey's wheat research and training project.* CIMMYT Today, no. 6. Mexico City: International Maize and Wheat Improvement Center. 18 pp.
  A highly readable and well-illustrated article on the Turkish wheat revolution.

Demir, Nazmi. 1976. *The adoption of new bread wheat technology in selected regions of Turkey.* Mexico City: International Maize and Wheat Improvement Center. 27 pp.
  An "adoption study" commissioned by the CIMMYT economics program to learn more about the circumstances of wheat farmers.

Humphrey, L. M. 1969. *Mexican wheat comes to Turkey.* Ankara: U.S. Agency for International Development. 68 pp.
  Traces the steps by which semi-dwarf wheats were introduced into the lowlands of Turkey during the late 1960s.

Mann, Charles K. 1977. The impact of technology on wheat production in Turkey. *Studies in development* (Middle East Technical University, Ankara) 14:30–46.
Presents Turkish wheat production statistics for 1946–1976 and analyzes the role of weather and some inputs (fertilizers, herbicides, tractors).

_____ . 1980. The effects of government policy on income distribution: A case study of wheat production in Turkey since World War II. In *Political economy of income distribution in Turkey*, ed. Ergun Ozbudun and Aydin Ulusan, pp. 197–245. New York: Holmes & Meier.
Assesses the distribution of benefits in the Turkish wheat revolution from usage of tractors, high-yielding wheat varieties, fertilizers, herbicides, tillage practices, and credit and comments on the income-distribution aspects of the government wheat-production programs.

Oregon State University. 1976. *USAID/OSU wheat research and production project in Turkey*. Corvallis. 89 pp.
Report on wheat research on the plateau of Turkey from 1969 to 1976.

Chapter 6. Bangladesh, China, Brazil, and Argentina

Anderson, R. G.; Saari, Eugene; Biggs, Stephen D.; Klatt, Art; Borlaug, Norman; Nasr, Hikmat; and Alcala, Max. 1978. The Bangladesh wheat expansion program. Mimeographed. Dacca: Bangladesh Agricultural Research Institute. 23 pp.
Reviews progress in wheat for 1977–1978 and gives program recommendations.

Bangladesh Rice Research Institute. 1977. *Workshop on ten years of modern rice and wheat cultivation in Bangladesh*. Dacca. 318 pp.
Nineteen technical papers, half dealing with wheat, including a 10-year plan for wheat, 1977–1987.

Clay, Edward J., ed. 1978. Ten years of dwarf wheat production in Bangladesh. Mimeographed. Dacca: Bangladesh Agricultural Research Council. 22 pp.
A compilation of data on area, yield, and production of wheat, 1966–1967 through 1977–1978, with bibliography.

International Fertilizer Development Center. 1978. *The Bangladesh fertilizer sector*. Muscle Shoals, Ala. 57 pp.

A survey of fertilizer production, bagging, warehousing, usage, prices, subsidies, and extension services.

Khan, Akhtar Hameed. 1974. *Reflections on the Comilla rural development projects.* Washington, D.C.: American Council on Education, Overseas Liaison Committee.
Reviews the program of the Comilla Academy, a rural development research and training center in Comilla, East Pakistan (now Bangladesh), of which Khan served as director, 1960–1971.

U.S., National Academy of Sciences. 1977. *Wheat in the People's Republic of China.* Washington, D.C. 190 pp.
A report by a delegation that visited China in 1976.

Chapter 7. Elements of an Effective National Wheat Program

Asian Development Bank. 1977. *Asian agricultural survey, 1976.* Manila. 490 pp.
Gives data and advice on many agricultural problems, including agricultural credit systems (pp. 259–261).

Benor, Daniel, and Harrison, James Q. 1977. *Agricultural extension: The training and visit system.* Washington, D.C.: World Bank. 55 pp.
Explains an extension procedure that is well adapted for developing countries.

Boyce, James K., and Evenson, Robert E. 1975. *National and international agricultural research and extension programs.* New York: Agricultural Development Council. 229 pp.
Analyzes expenditures on agricultural research and extension in more than 100 countries from 1959 to 1974.

Douglas, Johnson E., ed. 1980. *Successful seed programs: A planning and management guide.* Boulder, Colo.: Westview Press. 302 pp.
A comprehensive discussion of seed programs.

Moseman, Albert H., ed. 1971. *National agricultural research systems in Asia.* New York: Agricultural Development Council. 271 pp.
Proceedings of a seminar; describes the status of agricultural research in Asian countries.

Mosher, A. T. 1975. *Serving agriculture as an administrator.* New York: Agricultural Development Council. 64 pp.
Presents the principles of agricultural administration.

World Bank. 1975. *Agricultural credit: A sector policy paper.* Washington, D.C. 85 pp.

> Describes agricultural credit practices in the developing nations and gives statistical annexes on the scope of credit programs in various countries.

_____. 1975. *Rural development: A sector policy paper.* Washington, D.C. 89 pp.

> Explains the components of rural development in the developing countries.

Chapter 8. Postharvest Wheat Handling

FAO. 1977. *Analysis of an FAO survey of post-harvest food losses in developing countries.* Rome. 143 pp.

> An attempt to measure postharvest crop losses.

_____. 1979. *Processing and storage of foodgrains by rural families.* Rome. 214 pp.

> Describes improved practices for cereal threshing, winnowing, drying, storage, and pest control.

Inglett, George E., ed. 1974. *Wheat: Production and utilization.* Westport, Conn.: Avi Publishing. 500 pp.

> Focuses on postharvest technology including harvesting and storage, milling, baking, enrichment, feed and industrial uses, and the movement of wheat products in world trade.

Quisenberry, K. S., and Reitz, L. P., eds. 1967. *Wheat and wheat improvement.* Madison, Wis.: American Society of Agronomy. 560 pp.

> See annotation under Chapter 1.

Spicer, Arnold, ed. 1975. *Bread.* London: Applied Science Publishers. 358 pp.

> Contains 24 papers on wheat and wheat products. Its discussion of postharvest technology is especially useful.

Chapter 9. Promising Wheat Research for the Future

American Society of Agronomy. 1976. *Multiple cropping.* Madison, Wis. 378 pp.

> An authoritative book on multiple cropping, which is likely to play an increasing role in expanded food production.

_____ . 1978. *Crop tolerance to suboptimal land conditions*. Madison, Wis. 343 pp.
An important reference book for agricultural researchers.

Brown, A.W.A.; Byerly, T. C.; Gibbs, M.; and San Pietro, A., eds. 1975. *Crop productivity*. East Lansing: Michigan Agricultural Experiment Station and Charles F. Kettering Foundation. 400 pp.
Reports a conference on the priorities for agricultural research.

Byerlee, Derek, and Collinson, Michael. 1979. *On-farm research to develop technologies appropriate to farmers: The potential role of economists*. Mexico City: International Maize and Wheat Improvement Center. 8 pp.
Presents the case for on-farm research.

Hanson, Haldore, ed. 1979. Biological resources: Research and development strategies for the 1980s. Mimeographed. New York: Rockefeller Foundation. 75 pp.
Suggests priorities for agricultural research in the 1980s.

International Maize and Wheat Improvement Center. 1980. *CIMMYT looks ahead: A planning report for the 1980's*. Mexico City. 78 pp.
Outlines CIMMYT's research priorities.

_____ . 1980. *Planning technologies appropriate to farmers: Concepts and procedures*. Mexico City. 71 pp.
A manual for training economists and agronomists in the conduct of on-farm surveys.

Kern, Robert K. 1980. *Probing the gene pools*. CIMMYT Today, no. 12. Mexico City: International Maize and Wheat Improvement Center. 11 pp.
Describes the program for crossing winter-habit and spring-habit wheats in Mexico and at Oregon State University.

Lelley, J. 1976. *Wheat breeding*. Budapest: Hungarian Academy of Sciences. 286 pp.
A useful reference book for wheat breeders. Covers wheat genetics, breeding methods, major wheat characteristics, wheat diseases, and quality improvement.

Mertin, J. V. 1979. *Speeding the breeding*. CIMMYT Today, no. 11.

Mexico City: International Maize and Wheat Improvement Center.
15 pp.
  Explains the importance of off-season nurseries for wheat research
  and describes the operation of such nurseries in Mexico, India, Iran,
  Pakistan, Syria, and Kenya.

Perrin, R. K.; Winkelmann, Donald L.; Moscardi, Edgardo L.; and
Anderson, Jock R. 1976. *From agronomic data to farmer recommenda-*
tions: An economics training manual. Mexico City: International Maize
and Wheat Improvement Center. 51 pp.
  Prepared for training agricultural economists. Stresses conversion of
  agronomic data into recommendations to farmers.

Zeven, Anton C., and Zeven-Hissink, Nineke Ch. 1976. *Geneologies of*
14,000 wheat varieties. Wageningen: Netherlands Cereal Center and International Maize and Wheat Improvement Center. 120 pp.
  Lists pedigrees for both winter-habit and spring-habit wheats and for
  both bread wheats and durums.

Chapter 10. Prospects for Wheat in the 1980s and 1990s

Anderson, R. G. 1978. The aftermath of the green revolution. In *Cereals*
'78: Proceedings of the Sixth Cereal and Bread Conference, ed. Y.
Pomeranz, pp. 15–32. St. Paul, Minn.: American Association of Cereal
Chemists.
  A careful treatment of world population growth and the outlook for
  food supplies.

Borlaug, N. E. 1979. The magnitude and complexities of producing and
distributing equitably the food required for a population of four billion
which continues to grow at a frightening rate. In *Proceedings of the Fifth*
International Wheat Genetics Symposium, vol. 1. New Delhi: Indian
Council of Agricultural Research.
  Discusses the conflict between population growth and food supply in
  the 1970s and 1980s.

Brown, Lester R. 1974. *By bread alone.* New York: Praeger Publishers.
272 pp.
  An analysis of the world's food resources in relation to population
  growth.

FAO. 1979. *1978 fertilizer yearbook.* Vol. 23. Rome. 200 pp.

Contains data on fertilizer production, stocks, sales, consumption, and prices in most countries of the world. Part of an annual series.

_____ . 1980. *1979 trade yearbook*. Vol. 33. Rome. 357 pp.
Contains data on volume and value of agricultural products moving in international trade. Part of an annual series.

Population Reference Bureau. 1980. *1980 world population data sheet*. Washington, D.C. 2 pp.
Published annually.

Wortman, Sterling, and Cummings, Ralph W., Jr. 1978. *To feed this world*. Baltimore: Johns Hopkins University Press. 440 pp.
One of the most comprehensive and readable recent books on the world food situation.

Appendix: Where to Get Wheat Assistance

Consultative Group on International Agricultural Research (CGIAR). 1980. *International agricultural research*. Washington, D.C. 50 pp.
Describes the work of the 13 international agricultural centers and services supported by the CGIAR. It is useful for the administrator who wants to know the kinds of help obtainable from each center.

International Agricultural Development Service. 1980. *Agricultural assistance sources*. 3d ed. New York. 251 pp.
Describes the activities and interests of over 20 organizations that offer financial and technical assistance to developing countries.

International Maize and Wheat Improvement Center. 1979. *International testing program in wheat, triticale, and barley*. CIMMYT Today, no. 10. Mexico City. 15 pp.
A description of international nurseries distributed from Mexico; useful for governments interested in participating.

Wolff, A. 1978. *CIMMYT training*. CIMMYT Today, no. 9. Mexico City: International Maize and Wheat Improvement Center. 16 pp.
An illustrated account of the wheat and maize training programs at CIMMYT.

World Bank. 1976. *Questions and answers*. Washington, D.C. 71 pp.
Describes the kinds of projects in which the World Bank has a major interest and explains how to start negotiations.

Index

Acid soils, 28, 128
  in Africa and Asia, 82
  in Brazil, 79–81, 139
Afghanistan, 138
Africa, 23–24, 82
Agricultural companies
  assistance from, 154
Agronomic research, 22–23, 89–90
  in Bangladesh, 71
  in China, 78
  in India, 44–45
  in Mexico, 35–37
  in Turkey, 62–65
Agropyron, 140
Aleurone layer, 117
Algeria, 127, 136
Aluminum tolerance, 79–80, 89(table)
Amino acids, 11–12
Aphid, 36, 132
Area planted to wheat, by country,
  4–5(table)
Argentina, 82, 87, 125, 131, 136, 138,
  139, 148
Australia, 8–9, 16

Bakeries, commercial, 117–118
Bangladesh, 69–73. *See also* Demonstrations
  and trials, on-farm; Price supports
  for wheat
Borlaug, Norman E., 43
Bran in wheat, 12
Brazil, 16, 23, 79–82, 80(map), 88, 139
Bread wheat, 9
  varieties released by Mexico, 32(table)
Breeding. *See* Wheat breeding
Budgeting for national wheat program, 103
Bunt (*Tilletia spp.*), endemic areas and losses
  from, 120–121(table)
Burma, 82

Canada, 16
Chile, 125, 136, 138, 139
China, 74–78, 75(map), 87, 127, 136, 140
  area, yield, and production of wheat, 74
  fertilizer factories, 146
  land improvement, 75
  storage methods, 115–116
  See also Multiple cropping
Chinch bug, 132
CIMMYT. *See* International Maize and Wheat

Improvement Center
Cleaning wheat grain, 111
Club wheat, 9
Composite flour, 118
Couscous (steamed cracked wheat), 138
Credit, agricultural, 100–101
Crossing block
  at CIMMYT, 89(table)
  definition, 88
  for durum, 139

Day-length insensitivity, 22
Demonstrations and trials,
  on-farm, 90
  in Bangladesh, 72
  in India, 45, 47
Diseases of wheat, 23–26, 119–126
  in Brazil, 81
  in China, 74–75
  losses from, 119
  in Mexico, 37–39
  See also Rust diseases
Douglas, Johnson E., 93
Drainage, 95
Drying wheat grain, 111
Durum wheat, 9–10
  future research needs, 138–139
  varieties released by Mexico, 33
Dwarf wheat. *See* Semi-dwarf wheat

Early maturity, 20, 89(table)
Economists' role in wheat research. *See* Farm
  studies
Egypt, 17
Elymus, 140
Employment
  generated by modern wheats, 26
  in public works, 105
  off-farm, 27
Endosperm, 117
Environmental stress, 126–127
Erosion control, 95
Erysiphe graminis. See Powdery mildew
Export of wheat
  difficulties for developing countries, 104
  list of major marketers, 147(table)
Extension services
  agent training, 97
  demonstrations and field days, 98
  maintaining morale, 100

Facultative wheats, 10, 11
  in China, 74
  in Turkey, 61
FAO. *See* Food and Agricultural Organization
    of the United Nations
Farmers' service organizations, 106
  in Mexico, 39
Farm studies, 133–135
Feed wheat, 104
Fertilizer
  adjusting the formula for, 129
  efficient use of, 128–130
  feedstocks for production of, 145–146
  organic, 76, 129–130
  production outlook for, 144, 146
  response of semi-dwarf wheats to, 20
  response of traditional wheats to, 16
  role in wheat revolution, 93–94
  usage: in Bangladesh, 72; in China, 76; in
    India, 23, 50; in Turkey, 66; in world
    record yield, 7
  See also Micronutrients; Nitrogen;
    Phosphorus; Potassium
Food and Agricultural Organization of the
    United Nations (FAO), 113, 130
Food-for-work program, 105
Food reserves, 103
Foreign aid, 73, 151
France, 16
Fumigation of stored wheat, 114
Fungicides, 38, 96, 132
Fusarium spp. See Scab

Germ in wheat, 12
Germ-plasm banks, 128
  Fort Collins, Colorado, 126
  Vavilov Institute (USSR), 126
Glume blotch. *See* Septoria
Gluten, 1, 12. *See also* Protein in wheat grain
Grading wheat flour, 117
Green revolution, 26–28

Handling and transporting wheat, 112
Harvest index, 21
Harvesting operations, 109–110
Head blight. *See* Scab
Helminthosporium (root rot, seedling blight,
    leaf blight), 125–126
  endemic areas and losses from, 120–121
    (table)
  Helminthosporium gigantium, 126
  Helminthosporium sativum, 121, 125
  Helminthosporium tritici repentis, 126
Herbicides, 95–96, 131
  in Turkey, 64, 66(table)
Hessian fly, 132
Hordeum, 140

IADS. *See* International Agricultural
    Development Service
ICARDA. *See* International Center for
    Agricultural Research in Dry Areas

Imports of wheat
  by developing countries, 102, 147(table)
  future outlook for, 146
  by Mexico, 42
India, 16, 22–23, 26, 27, 28, 46(map), 87, 99
  agricultural universities, 51–52
  agronomy trials, 44
  controversies over wheat technology,
    52–54
  demonstration of new wheats, 45, 47
  fertilizer factories, 51
  Indian Agricultural Research Institute, 45
  multilines released by, 123
  potential wheat production, 56
  seed imports, 47
  storage of grain, 54–55
  Tarai Development Corporation, 54
  value of increased wheat yield, 57
  wheat breeding, 48–49
  wheat yields, 56
  yield gap between researcher and farmer,
    128
Indonesia, 82
Industrial uses of wheat, 105
INIA. *See* National Institute of Agricultural
    Research, Mexico
Inputs for wheat crop, 92–97
  subsidy of, 102
  See also Fertilizer; Irrigation;
    Mechanization; Pesticides; Seed
    multiplication
Insecticides, 132
Insects, 132
INTA. *See* National Institute of Agricultural
    Technology, Argentina
International Agricultural Development
    Service (IADS), 151
International Center for Agricultural
    Research in Dry Areas (ICARDA), 15,
    16, 127
  activities of, 153–154
International Maize and Wheat
    Improvement Center (CIMMYT), xiv,
    15, 87, 127
  activities of, 151–153
Iran, 136, 138
Iraq, 138
Irrigation
  in Bangladesh, 72
  in China, 76
  importance of, 94–95
  in India, 23, 45, 50
  in Mexico, 30(map)
  in Pakistan, 50
  in world record yield, 7
Irrigation systems, design of, 95
Italy, 16

Kenya, 16, 31, 82, 123–124, 139

Land races, 17, 24, 29
Leaf blight. *See* Helminthosporium
Leaf blotch. *See* Septoria

Leaf rust (*Puccinia recondita*)
  endemic areas and losses from,
    120–121(table)
  resistance of parental varieties, 89(table)
  See also Rust diseases
Loans to farmers. *See* Credit, agricultural
Locust, giant, 132
Lodging, 16, 17(photo), 20
Loose smut (*Ustilago tritici*)
  endemic areas and losses from,
    120–121(table)
Lysine
  in maize, sorghum, and barley, 12
  See also Amino acids

Machinery. *See* Mechanization
Malaysia, 82
Marketing wheat
  export trade, 104, 112, 146–148
  import trade, 102
  international freight rates, 148
  local trade, 112
  See also Export of wheat; Imports of
    wheat
Mechanization
  for harvesting and threshing, 110–111
  in India, 51
  for short wheats, 97
  in Turkey, 62
Mexico, xiv, 6, 7–8, 15, 16, 18, 19, 23, 87
  agronomy practices, 35
  area, production, and yield of wheat,
    1946–1980, 34(fig.)
  farmers' service organization (Patronato),
    39
  imports of wheat grain, 42
  leaf rust epidemic, 1976–1977, 37
  potential wheat yields, 42
  research program, 30
  seed multiplication, 35
  training of wheat scientists, 39
  value of increased wheat, 40
  wheat varieties released, 32, 33(tables)
Micronutrients, 36, 128
Microplots, 50
Millfeeds, 117
Milling wheat, 116–117
Modern wheat. *See* Semi-dwarf wheat
Mozambique, 82
Multiline, 122–123
Multiple cropping, 144
  in China, 77

National Institute of Agricultural Research
    (INIA), Mexico, xiv, 30, 39
National Institute of Agricultural
    Technology (INTA), Argentina, 82
Nebraska, University of, 12, 154
Network of wheat scientists, 15, 150, 152
  definition of, 83, 85
Nitrogen, 7, 36
  deficiency of, 128
  losses from soil, 129

organic sources of, 129–130
  response of modern wheats, 20, 93–94
  response of tall wheats, 16
Nurseries
  CIMMYT, 152
  definition of, 83
  ICARDA, 153
  International Septoria Observation
    Nursery, 125
  International Spring Wheat Rust Nursery,
    154
  International Winter Wheat Performance
    Nursery, 154
  Tropical Helminthosporium Screening
    Nursery, 126
  Winter x Spring Wheat Screening Nursery,
    154
Nutritional benefits of modern wheat, 27

Oregon State University, 136, 154
Organic fertilizer, 129–130
  in China, 76
Oversupply of wheat, remedies, 103–106

Pakistan, 28, 49–52, 87
  increased wheat production, 50
  potential wheat production, 51, 56–57
  seed imports, 49
Patronato. *See* Mexico, farmers' service
    organization
People's Republic of China. *See* China
Pesticides, 95–97
Phosphorus, 7, 36, 79, 128, 129
Pinstrup-Andersen, Per, 93
Population
  future growth in wheat- producing
    countries, 142(table)
  pressure on land, 143–145
  world growth, 141
Postharvest operations. *See* Bakeries,
    commercial; Cleaning wheat grain;
    Composite flour; Drying wheat grain;
    Handling and transporting wheat;
    Harvesting operations; Marketing wheat;
    Milling wheat; Stored grain; Threshing
Potassium, 7, 36, 128
Powdery mildew (*Erysiphe graminis*)
  endemic areas and losses, 120–121(table)
  resistance of triticale, 139
Price supports for wheat, 101
  in Bangladesh, 73
  in India, 55
Production. *See* Wheat production
Protein in wheat grain, 2(table), 3, 11–12, 13
  increase of parent varieties, 89(table)
  See also Amino acids; Lysine
Puccinia graminis. See Stem rust
Puccinia recondita. See Leaf rust
Puccinia striiformis. See Stripe rust
Pustules, 24

Quarantine service, 91

Rhodesia. *See* Zimbabwe
Rockefeller Foundation, xiv
Root rot. *See* Helminthosporium
Rust diseases
  causes of, 24
  chemical sprays against, 25
  control of: by geographic placement of
    varieties, 124; by multilines, 122; by
    resistant varieties, 122; by varietal
    mixture, 123
  description of, 122
  epidemics of, 23, 37
  warning system against, 25
  See also Leaf rust; Stem rust; Stripe rust

Saline soil, 127
Scab (*Fusarium spp.,* head blight), 81, 125
  in China, 74
  endemic areas and losses, 120–121(table)
Scobie, Grant, 26
Seed imports
  by Bangladesh, 72
  by China, 76
  by India, 47
  by Pakistan, 49
  by Turkey, 62
Seedling blight. *See* Helminthosporium
Seed multiplication
  in Bangladesh, 72
  importance of, in rust control, 25
  in India, 45, 54
  ineffective programs, 92–93
  in Mexico, 35
Semi-dwarf wheat
  characteristics, 20–22
  development, 18–20
  new agronomic management, 22–23
  social impact, 26–28
Septoria (glume blotch), 81, 124, 136
  endemic areas and losses, 120–121(table)
  resistance of parental varieties, 89
  Septoria nodorum, 125
  Septoria tritici, 120–121(table), 136, 139
Shuttle breeding, 80
Slow rusting, 122
Soviet Union, 17
Soybean-wheat rotation, 81, 82
Species of wheat, 9
Spring-habit wheat
  characteristics, 10–11
  in China, 74
  in Turkey, 61, 62
Spring wheat. *See* Spring-habit wheat
Spring x winter crosses, 135–136, 154
Stem rust (*Puccinia graminis*)
  endemic areas and losses, 120–121(table)
  resistance of parental varieties, 89(table)
  See also Rust diseases
Stored grain
  in Bangladesh, 73
  in China, 115–116
  control of moisture, 115
  in food reserve, 103

  fungi, 114
  in India, 54, 116
  insects, 114
  in Turkey, 116
Stripe rust (*Puccinia striiformis*)
  effect of spring-winter crosses, 136
  endemic areas and losses, 120–121(table)
  resistance of parental varieties, 89(table)
  See also Rust diseases
Subsidies of food, 102
Subsidies of inputs, 102
Substitute crops for wheat, 105
Sulfur, 128
Sunnipest. *See* Chinch bug
Surplus wheat. *See* Oversupply of wheat,
  remedies

Tanzania, 82, 139
Tarai Development Corporation, 54
Thailand, 82
Threshing, 109–110
Tillers, 16, 20
Tilletia spp. See Bunt
Trade in wheat. *See* Marketing wheat
Traditional wheats, 16–18
Training wheat scientists
  for Bangladesh, 71
  at CIMMYT, 152
  at ICARDA, 153–154
  for India, 51
  for Mexico, 39
  for Pakistan, 49, 52
  for Turkey, 66
Trap nurseries, 90
Trials, on-farm. *See* Demonstrations and
  trials, on-farm
Triticale, 139
Triticum aestivum, 9
Triticum compactum, 9
Triticum durum, 9
Tunisia, 7
Turkey, 28, 60(map), 87, 131, 136, 138
  environments for wheat, 59–61
  fertilizer use, 66
  herbicide use, 66
  mechanization, 62, 66(table)
  potential wheat production, 67–68
  revolution of wheat, 61–65
  seed imports, 62
  sheep and wheat competition, 17
  stockpile of wheat, 67
  weather, 65
  yield, area, and production of wheat,
    66(fig.)

United Kingdom, 8
United States Department of Agriculture, 154
Ustilago tritici. See Loose smut

Varietal improvement. *See* Wheat breeding
Varietal mixture, 123–124
Vavilov Institute (USSR), 126
Vernalization, 10, 135

Warning system against disease pathogens, 25, 90
Washington State University, 18–19
Weed control
  by chemicals, 131
  by cropping systems, 131
  by hand pulling, 130
  by integrated systems, 132
Wheat breeding
  for day-length insensitivity, 22
  for disease resistance, 23–25, 119–123
  for durum improvement, 138–139
  for dwarfing, 18
  for early maturity, 120
  for higher harvest index, 21
  for lodging resistance, 20
  for longer heads and more spikelets, 137–138
  for multiline development, 122–123
  for spring-winter crosses, 135–136
  for tolerance to environmental stress, 126–127
  by two cycles a year, 31
  for wide adaptation, 22
  for wide crosses, 139
Wheat production, 3, 4–5(table)
  in Bangladesh, 70(table)
  in China, 74
  future world prospects, 148–150
  in India, 56
  in Mexico, 29
  in Pakistan, 50
  in Turkey, 66(table)
Wheat qualities, 13
Wheat research. *See* Agronomic research; Demonstrations and trials, on-farm; Farm studies; Wheat breeding
Wheat technology laboratory, 90–91
Wheat types, 9–11. *See also* Bread wheat; Club wheat; Durum wheat; Facultative wheats; Species of wheat; Spring-habit wheat; Winter-habit wheat
Wheat varieties
  Alondra, 80
  Arjun, 48
  Bezostaya, 63
  Blue Silver, 51
  Bolal, 63
  Daruma, 18
  Frontera, 31, 209
  Fultz, 18
  Gaines, 18

INIA 66, 71
Jupateco 73, 37, 38, 71
Kalyansona, 48, 71
Kavkaz, 136
Lerma Rojo, 43, 45, 62, 64
Marco Juarez INTA, 82
Norin 10, 17, 18, 19, 20
Norin 10-Brevor, 18
Pavon 76, 71, 122
Penjamo 62, 19, 43, 122
Pitic 62, 19, 43
Siete Cerros, 49
Sonalika, 48, 71
Sonora 64, 43, 45, 62, 71
Super-X, 49
Supremo 211, 31
Taishan 1, 4, and 5, 76
Tanori, 71
Tetrastichun, 137
Thatcher, 135
Torim 73, 122
Veery, 136
Wheat yields, 3, 4–5(table)
  environmental effects, 3–8
  increase by countries, 4–5(table)
  world record, 17
Wide adaptation, 22
Wide crosses, 139
Winter-habit wheat, 1
  characteristics, 10–11
  in China, 74
  in Turkey, 59
Winter x spring crosses. *See* Spring x winter crosses
Winter wheat. *See* Winter-habit wheat
World Bank, 26

Yellow berry, 138
Yield. *See* Wheat yields
Yield gap, 127–128
Yield potentials
  future expansion: in China, 78; in India, 56; in Mexico, 42; in Pakistan, 57; in Turkey, 67
  methods to increase, 135
  Mexican bread wheats, 32(table)
  Mexican durum wheats, 33(table)

Zaire, 82
Zambia, 82
Zimbabwe, 17, 82
Zinc, 128